PREFACE TO [illegible]

Since the publication of the sec[illegible] *and Policy* in May 1997, no one monument[illegible] immigration landscape. But there have been hundreds of smaller yet significant developments in the legislative, administrative, judicial, political, and academic arenas. Hence, this Supplement.

The vast bulk of the material presented here modifies existing material. The one major exception is a new section on the Convention Against Torture (chapter 9, new section C).

This Supplement is intended to be current through June 1999.

I renew my thanks to the many people already acknowledged in the Prefaces to the first and second editions. Here I add my deep appreciation to Susan Saab Fortney, Elwin Griffith, David Hudson, Estelle Lau, Daniel Levy, and Victor Romero.

This Supplement is dedicated to the memory of a remarkable man. Charles Gordon died this past spring. He was larger than life -- a true pioneer, a wonderful colleague, and above all else, a mensch.

Steve Legomsky
St. Louis
June 1999

1999 SUPPLEMENT

to

Second Edition of

IMMIGRATION AND REFUGEE LAW AND POLICY

Stephen H. Legomsky

**Charles F. Nagel Professor
of International and Comparative Law**

Washington University

extra class
May 2

ISBN 1–56662–833–4

TEXT IS PRINTED ON 10% POST
CONSUMER RECYCLED PAPER

SUMMARY OF CONTENTS

TABLE OF CASES

[Note: This Table lists all cases that are cited in this Supplement, except for those that are cited only in reprinted materials. References are to pages of the Supplement.]

TABLE OF AUTHORITIES

[This Table lists all books, articles (other than newspaper articles), and reports cited in this Supplement, except for those that are cited only within reprinted materials. Student Notes and Comments are alphabetized under "Note."]

Gyory, Andrew, Closing the Gate -- Race, Politics, and the Chinese Exclusion Act (1998) 2

Hammar, Tomas, Democracy and the Nation State (1990) 104

Hathaway, James C., The Law of Refugee Status (1991) 95

Hathaway, James C. & Neve, R. Alexander, *Making International Refugee Law Relevant Again: A Proposal for Collectivized and Solution-Oriented Protection*, 10 Harv. Human Rights J. 115 (1997) 57

Helton, Arthur C. & Nicoll, Alison, *Female Genital Mutilation as Ground for Asylum in the United States: The Recent Case of In re Fauziya Kasinga and Prospects for More Gender Sensitive Approaches*, 28 Colum. Human Rights L. Rev. 375 (1997) . . 66

Hernandez-Truyol, Berta Esperanza, *Borders (En)gendered: Normativities, Latinas, and the LatCrit Paradigm*, 72 NYU L. Rev. 882 (1997) 13

Hernandez-Truyol, Berta Esperanza & Johns, Kimberly A., *Global Rights, Local Wrongs, and Legal Fixes: An International Human Rights Critique of Immigration and Welfare "Reform"*, 71 So. Cal. L. Rev. 547 (1998) 101

Hirson, David & Mayou, Catherine I., *The Sinking of the Titanic or the Rising of the Phoenix? - An Update on Immigrant Investor Visas*, September 1998 Immigration Briefings 12

Hopper, Robert & Osuna, Juan P., *Remedies of Last Resort: Private Bills and Deferred Action*, June 1997 Immigration Briefings 41,42

Horne, Daniel C. & Weitzhandler, L. Ari, *Asylum Law after the Illegal Immigration Reform and Immigrant Responsibility Act*, April 1997 Immigration Briefings . . . 27

Hudson, David M., *Tax Problems for Departing Aliens*, March 1997 Immigration Briefings 105

Inniss, Lolita Buckner, *Dutch Uncle Sam: Immigration Reform and Notions of Family*, 36 Brandeis J. Family L. 177 (1997-98) 12

Innis, Lolita Buckner, *The Legacy of Racially Restrictive Immigration Laws and Policies and the Construction of the American National Identity*, 76 Oreg. L. Rev. 369 (1997) 13

Neuman, Gerald L., *Aliens as Outlaws: Government Services, Proposition 187, and the Structure of Equal Protection Doctrine*, 42 UCLA L. Rev. 1425 (1995) 96,101

Neuman, Gerald L., *Habeas Corpus, Executive Detention, and the Removal of Aliens*, 98 Colum. L. Rev. 961 (1998) 54

Osuna, Juan P. (ed.), Understanding the 1996 Immigration Act (1997) 1

Osuna, Juan P. & Mariani, Patricia, *Expedited Removal: Authorities, Implementation, and Ongoing Policy and Practice Issues*, Nov. 1997 Immigration Briefings . . . 71

Palmer, Gary W., *Guarding the Coast: Alien Migrant Interdiction Operations at Sea*, 29 Conn. L. Rev. 1565 (1997) 73

Papademetriou, Demetrios, Aleinikoff, T. Alexander, & Meyers, Deborah, Reorganizing the U.S. Immigration Function: Toward a New Framework for Accountability (1998), reproduced in 75 Interpreter Releases 501 (Apr. 13, 1998) 1

Pilcher, Susan L., *Justice without a Blindfold: Criminal Proceedings and the Alien Defendant*, 50 Arkansas L. Rev. 269 (1997) 32

Ragland, Thomas K., *Presumed Incredible: A View from the Dissent*, 75 Interpreter Releases 1541 (Nov. 9, 1998) 67

Reich, Peter L., *Environmental Metaphor in the Alien Benefits Debate*, 42 U.C.L.A. L.Rev. 1577 (1995) 101

Rizza, Nicholas J., *INS Detention: The Impact on Asylum Seekers*, 17 Refugee Rpts. No. 8, at 2 (Aug. 30, 1996) 72

Romero, Victor C., *Expanding the Circle of Membership by Reconstructing the "Alien": Lessons from Social Psychology and the "Promise Enforcement" Cases*, 32 Univ. Mich. Journal of Law Reform 1, 20-34 (1998) 32

Romero, Victor C., *The Congruence Principle Applied: Rethinking Equal Protection Review of Federal Alienage Classifications after Adarand Constructors, Inc. v. Pena*, 76 Oreg. L. Rev. 425 (1997) 96,102

Romero, Victor C., *Whatever Happened to the Fourth Amendment? Undocumented Immigrants' Rights after INS v. Lopez-Mendoza and United States v. Verdugo-Urquidez*, 65 So. Cal. L. Rev. 999 (1992) 50

Wettstein, Nadine, *The Peddler Sells His Caps: The EOIR and INS Issue a New Rule on the Suspension/Cancellation Ceiling*, 3 Bender's Immigration Bulletin 1083 (Nov. 1, 1998) 36,40

Wheeler, Charles, *Affidavit of Support: A Year in Review*, 4 Bender's Immigration Bulletin 97 (Feb. 1, 1999) 21

Wheeler, Charles, *The Affidavit of Support and Sponsorship Requirements: A Critical Analysis*, June 1998 Immigration Briefings 21

Wheeler, Charles & McClenahan, Mary, *C.L.I.N.I.C. Report # 4 on Credible Fear / Expedited Removal* (Oct. 29, 1997) 70-71

Wheeler, Charles & McClenehan, Mary, *C.L.I.N.I.C. Report # 5 on Credible Fear / Expedited Removal*, 3 Bender's Immigration Bulletin 411 (May 1, 1998) 70,72

Women's Commission for Refugee Women and Children, An Uncertain Future, A Cruel Present: Women in INS Detention (1996) 72

Women's Commission for Refugee Women and Children, Liberty Denied: Women Seeking Asylum Imprisoned in the United States (April 1997) 72

Wood, Charles, *Losing Control of America's Future -- The Census, Birthright Citizenship, and Illegal Aliens*, 22 Harv. J. L. & Pub. Policy 465 (1999) 100

Yale-Loehr, Stephen, *Beating the Bar: Avoiding, Delaying or Remedying Unlawful Presence*, 3 Bender's Immigration Bulletin 779 (Aug. 1, 1998) 19

OVERVIEW CHAPTER

Page 2, after the first paragraph, insert two new paragraphs:

For many years, calls have been made to separate the INS into two agencies -- one for enforcement and one for service. The U.S. Commission on Immigration Reform, appointed by Congress to perform a comprehensive study of United States immigration and nationality policy, in 1997 proposed a sweeping reorganization of the executive branch immigration functions. See U.S. Commission on Immigration Reform, Becoming an American: Immigration and Immigrant Policy 148-83 (1997).

Several thoughtful commentators and government officials offered counterproposals. See, e.g., Gene McNary, *No Authority, No Accountability: Don't Abolish the INS, Make It an Independent Agency*, 74 Interpreter Releases 1281 (Aug. 25, 1997); Demetrios Papademetriou, T. Alexander Aleinikoff & Deborah Meyers, Reorganizing the U.S. Immigration Function: Toward a New Framework for Accountability (1998), reproduced in 75 Interpreter Releases 501 (Apr. 13, 1998); Cornelius D. Scully, *Reorganizing the Administration of the Immigration Laws: Recommendations and Historical Context*, 75 Interpreter Releases 937 (July 13, 1998). Congress has held hearings on the issue. At this writing, no resolution has been reached.

Page 2, 2nd current paragraph, add at end:

Juan P. Osuna (ed.), Understanding the 1996 Immigration Act (1997).

CHAPTER 1

IMMIGRATION AND THE CONSTITUTION

Page 1, footnote 1, column 2, line 3, before the Frank Wu citation, add:

Linda Kelly, *Preserving the Fundamental Right to Family Unity: Championing Notions of Social Contract and Community Ties in the Battle of Plenary Power versus Aliens' Rights*, 41 Villanova L. Rev. 725 (1996).

Page 12, middle of page, after Chuman citation:

Professor Natsu Taylor Saito, in *Alien and Non-Alien Alike: Citizenship, "Foreignness", and Racial Hierarchy in American Law*, 76 Oreg. L. Rev. 261 (1997), observes that in the United States discrimination against persons of Asian descent has historically engulfed both United States citizens and aliens. She suggests that other Americans often view Asian-Americans as perpetual "foreigners." Accord, Kevin R. Johnson, *Racial Hierarchy, Asian Americans and Latinos as "Foreigners" and Social Change: Is Law the Way to Go?*, 76 Oreg. L. Rev. 347 (1997).

Page 16, at end of item 4, add a new paragraph:

Professor Maria Frankowska (in correspondence with the author) poses an intriguing question. She asks whether Congress's power is "plenary" not only as against the courts, but also as against the President. If so, she then points out, it would be difficult to derive the congressional power from the general foreign affairs power, which Congress clearly shares with the President. Perhaps, then, the power is "plenary" only as against the courts. This interpretation would also square with the reference, at the end of the Supreme Court's opinion in the *Chinese Exclusion Case*, to the "political" branch of the government. That reference is broad enough to encompass both Congress and the President.

Page 20, next-to-last paragraph, before Hing citation, add:

Andrew Gyory, Closing the Gate -- Race, Politics, and the Chinese Exclusion Act (1998) (a political history of the Act); Lucy Salyer, Laws Harsh as Tigers: Chinese Immigrants and the Shaping of Modern Immigration Law (1995); Estelle T. Lau, *Excavating the "Chinese Wall": Towards a Socio-Historical Perspective on the Development of United States Immigration Administration and Chinese Exclusion*, 92

Northwestern Univ. L. Rev. 1068 (1998) (book review of Salyer).

Page 23, middle of page, after Spiro citation, add:

Peter J. Spiro, *Learning to Live with Immigration Federalism*, 29 Conn. L. Rev. 1627 (1997) (arguing "steam-valve" theory -- allowing greater state control would confine effects of anti-immigrant sentiment to affected states, rather than spur national legislation).

Page 24, after 3rd full paragraph, add new paragraph:

A brief word on organization: Immigration officials make a range of important decisions in individual cases. As you will see in chapter 8, IIRAIRA contained several provisions that bar or restrict judicial review of many of these. Several courts have now addressed both the meaning and the constitutionality of some of those provisions. These cases are discussed in the judicial review section of chapter 8, rather than in chapter 1.

Page 62, before subsection b, add a new paragraph:

The problem of "nonremovable detainees" usually arises either because the person's country of nationality will not accept his or her return or because the United States does not have diplomatic relations with that country. If a person has been ordered removed but the order cannot be executed, and the INS believes the person is dangerous, the choice between release and continued indefinite detention is a difficult one. As of September 1998, the INS was indefinitely detaining approximately 2500 nonremovable people. A majority are from from Cuba, but there are significant numbers from Vietnam, Cambodia, and Laos as well. 3 Bender's Immigration Bulletin 1098 (Nov. 1, 1998). Another 1000 are in federal custody serving criminal sentences. *Id.* On April 30, 1999, the INS announced it would individually review each case to determine whether the person could safely be released. Patricia Zengerle, *U.S. to Review Immigrants' Indefinite Detention*, Reuters (Apr. 30, 1999).

Page 80, after last full paragraph, add the following:

In February 1999, the Supreme Court decided *Reno v. American-Arab Anti-Discrimination Committee*, 119 S.Ct. 936 (1999). The INS had brought removal proceedings against eight aliens. Two of them, both lawful permanent residents, were charged with supporting the Popular Front for the Liberation of Palestine, an organization alleged to advocate various terrorist acts. The other six were charged with overstaying their visas. All eight sought to enjoin the removal proceedings on the ground that the government had selectively targeted them because of their membership in the PFLP. They argued that the selective prosecution violated their First Amendment rights to free speech and free association.

The Supreme Court had granted certiorari to decide whether recent legislation eliminated the lower courts' power to hear the case before the issuance of final removal orders. The Court ultimately held jurisdiction was lacking. That portion of the Court's opinion is discussed in chapter 8 of this Supplement. In the process of deciding the jurisdictional issue, however, the majority declared that "an alien unlawfully in this country has no constitutional right to assert selective enforcement as a defense against his deportation." 119 S.Ct. at 945. In a nearby footnote, the Court, possibly unintentionally, used even broader language. It said "Our holding generally deprives *deportable* aliens of the defense of selective prosecution [emphasis added]." *Id.* at 946 n.10. The latter language, if interpreted literally, would deny this defense even to lawfully admitted permanent resident aliens.

The Court offered several reasons for barring selective prosecution claims in removal proceedings. It suggested that the delay caused by such claims would cause special problems in the removal context, both because aliens have an inherent incentive to delay removal hearings and because delay permits "a continuing violation of United States law." In addition, the Court said, disclosure of the prosecution's reasons for prosecuting could expose sensitive foreign policy strategies. Finally, it was suggested, deportation is not punishment, and therefore the individual interest is less compelling than in a criminal case. 119 S.Ct. at 946-47.

Possible limitations on the Court's holding should be considered. The Court did not go so far as to bar all First Amendment claims in removal hearings. Most likely it did not mean to do so, since its rationales were specific to selective prosecution. Moreover, the Court expressly left open the possibility that a prosecution could reflect discrimination "so outrageous that the foregoing considerations can be overcome." 119 S.Ct. at 947. It concluded by saying "When an alien's continuing presence in this country is in violation of the immigration laws," selective prosecution based on membership of an organization that supports terrorist activity is permissible. *Id.* The repeated references to continuing presence might well mean that the Court did not intend to bar lawful permanent residents from asserting selective prosecution claims; their continuing presence would not violate the immigration laws. Justice Souter, dissenting, characterized the Court's conclusions about selective prosecution as dictum, since the Court ultimately found a lack of subject matter jurisdiction.

Page 80, last paragraph:

Delete the first clause, and begin the sentence with the phrase "Two leading exclusion cases . . ."

Page 82, after 1st full paragraph, add two new paragraphs:

Consider also whether retroactive deportation provisions might ever violate substantive due process. For a strong argument along those lines, see Nancy Morawetz, *Rethinking Retroactive Deportation Laws and the Due Process Clause*, 73 NYU L. Rev. 97 (1998).

10. With all the foregoing emphasis on *judicial* interpretation of the Constitution, it is important to remember that every member of Congress is also "bound by oath or affirmation, to support [the] Constitution." U.S. Const. art. VI, § 3. For a cogent reminder of this obligation in the immigration context, see Michael Scaperlanda, *Who is My Neighbor? An Essay on Immigrants, Welfare Reform, and the Constitution*, 29 Conn. L. Rev. 1587 (1997).

Page 89, at end of item 5, add a new paragraph:

In *Parra v. Perryman*, 172 F.3d 954 (7th Cir. 1999), one court held that the mandatory detention of aggravated felons during removal proceedings under new INA § 236(c) does not violate due process, at least when the person has "little hope" of avoiding ultimate removal. *Id.* at 958. Weeks later, another court reached the opposite conclusion, holding mandatory detention under section 236(c) violative of both substantive and procedural due process. *Van Eeton v. Beebe*, CV 99-16-PA (D. Oreg., Apr. 13, 1999).

Page 89, after item 6, add a new paragraph:

6A. For a strong argument that today's Supreme Court would not uphold explicit racial discrimination even in an immigration statute, see Gabriel J. Chin, *Segregation's Last Stronghold: Race Discrimination and the Constitutional Law of Immigration*, 46 UCLA L. Rev. 1 (1998).

Page 97, at end of 2nd full paragraph, add:

See also Richard Klein, *Immigration Laws as Instruments of Discrimination: Legislation Designed to Limit Chinese Immigration into the United Kingdom*, 7 Touro International L. Rev. 1 (1997).

CHAPTER 2

IMMIGRANT CATEGORIES

Page 99, 3rd paragraph, replace last sentence with:

An immigrant receives a so-called "green card" (which actually has changed colors many times over the years), now officially known as a "permanent resident" card. 63 Fed. Reg. 70,313 (Dec. 21, 1998). It is plastic and about the size of a credit card.

Page 110, top paragraph, line 4:

Change "admitting and expelling" to "excluding and expelling (now 'removing')."

Page 110, top paragraph, add at end:

See generally Juan P. Osuna, Understanding the 1996 Immigration Act (1997).

Page 116, item 1, after Carens citation, add:

Howard F. Chang, *Immigration Policy, Liberal Principles, and the Republican Tradition*, 85 Georgetown L.J. 2105 (1997) (history of immigration restrictions generally, and discriminatory immigration restrictions in particular, are incompatible with liberal principles of political theory on which republic was based).

Page 125, 2nd paragraph:

An error: In the line for (family-sponsored) first preference, insert the word "unmarried" before "sons and daughters."

Page 132, 2nd paragraph, replace 2nd and 3rd sentences with the following:

For example, the chart below shows that family-sponsored 3rd preference Mexicans who began the process on November 8, 1990 received visas in June 1999. They waited almost 9 years.

Pages 132-33, replace Visa Bulletin chart with the following:

UNITED STATES DEPARTMENT OF STATE, VISA BULLETIN
JUNE 1999

	All Areas Except Those Listed	CHINA-mainland born	INDIA	MEXICO	PHILIP-PINES
FAMILY PREFERENCES					
1st	15FEB98	15FEB98	15FEB98	08AUG93	22AUG87
2A*	22DEC94	22DEC94	22DEC94	22NOV93	22DEC94
2B	08JUL92	08JUL92	08JUL92	22JUL91	08JUL92
3rd	01AUG95	01AUG95	01AUG95	08NOV90	01JUL87
4th	22JUL88	22JUL88	15AUG86	01APR88	15JAN79
EMPLOYMENT PREFERENCES					
1st	C	01JUL98	C	C	C
2nd	C	22MAY97	08JAN98	C	C
3rd	C	15MAY95	15MAY96	C	C
Other Workers	01NOV92	01NOV92	01NOV92	01NOV92	01NOV92
4th	C	C	C	C	C
Certain Religious Workers	C	C	C	C	C
5th	C	C	C	C	C
Targeted Employment	C	C	C	C	C

Page 133, Problems, 1st line, replace "December 1996" with "June 1999."

Page 133, Problem 2, line 4:

Change "United States citizen" to "citizen and resident of the United States."

Page 141, at end of item 9, add a postscript:

On remand, a Hawaii trial court found that the state had no compelling interest in banning same-sex marriages, *Baehr v. Miike*, Civ. No. 91-1394, 1996 Westlaw 694235 (Haw. Cir. Ct., Dec. 3, 1996), and the Hawaii Supreme Court affirmed without a published opinion, 87 Haw. 34, 950 P.2d 1234 (Dec. 19, 1997). But the victory was short-lived. On November 3, 1998, the Hawaii voters passed a state constitutional amendment that prohibited same-sex marriages. Sam Howe Verhovek, *The 1998 Elections: The States -- Initiatives*, New York Times, Nov. 5, 1998, at B1. On the same day, Alaska voters took similar action. *Id.* As of March 11, 1999, some 29 states had expressly banned same-sex marriages. Al Knight, *Same-Sex Marriage: Losing War*, Denver Post, Mar. 11, 1999, at B-7. In the year 2000 an initiative to ban same-sex marriages will also appear on the California ballot. *Id.*

Page 146, item 5, add at end:

That is the the recent trend in Canada and western Europe. See, e.g., Citizenship and Immigration Canada, Building on a Strong Foundation for the 21st Century: New Directions for Immigration and Refugee Policy and Legislation at 25 (Jan. 1999) (proposing to admit same-sex partners); Lesbian and Gay Immigration Rights Task Force, Task Force Update (Summer 1998) at 1, 4 (reporting on recent implementing legislation in France and Belgium, and proposals in France), 2 (pre-election promise by now Chancellor Gerhard Schroeder to admit homosexual partners to Germany).

Page 159, after 4, add a new paragraph:

5. IMFA also made a fraudulent immigration marriage a criminal offense. For a strong argument against criminalizing selected marriages, see Maria Isabel Medina, *The Criminalization of Immigration Law: Employer Sanctions and Marriage Fraud*, 5 George Mason L. Rev. 669, 696-717 (1997).

Page 165, before the Problems, add:

8. Modern reproductive technology has raised some difficult issues as to how various family relationships should be defined for immigration purposes. For an intriguing exploration, see Bernard Friedland & Valerie Epps, *The Changing Family and the U.S. Immigration Laws: The Impact of Medical Reproductive Technology on the Immigration and Nationality Act's Definition of the Family*, 11 Georgetown Immigration L.J. 429 (1997).

Page 167, after 1st full paragraph, add:

In fiscal year 1998, Americans adopted 13,621 foreign children. Russia became the leading source country for American adoptions. After Russia, in order, came China, South Korea, Guatemala, and Romania. Chinese legislation passed in November 1998 liberalized the rules for foreign adoptions; increases are therefore likely. Renee Schoof, *Many U.S. Couples Adopting Abroad*, Associated Press (Jan. 9, 1999).

The conditions that turn foreign children into orphans remain distressing. AIDS alone has produced almost 8 million African orphans, many of whom are themselves HIV-positive. In China, a combination of population control and cultural preferences for boys has created a large population of orphaned baby girls. See Schoof, above.

Page 168, after 3rd paragraph, add:

On May 29, 1993, the Hague Conference on Private International Law adopted the Convention on Protection of Children and Co-Operation in Respect of Intercountry Adoption. The text is reproduced in 32 I.L.M. at 1139-46 (1993). The purpose of the Convention is to balance two sometimes conflicting goals -- facilitating international adoption of orphaned children and preventing child abduction, especially from third world countries. As of June 1998, thirty-two countries, including the United States, have signed the Convention. Seventeen have ratified it. President Clinton has submitted the Convention to the Senate for ratification. See White House Press Release (June 11, 1998), reproduced on the web at http://travel.state.gov/white_house.html. See also Adam Edward Rothwell, International Adoption, unpublished student seminar paper, on file with author (April 1999).

Page 169, 3rd full paragraph, add at end:

Accord, Enid Trucios-Haynes, *"Family Values" 1990s Style: U.S. Immigration Reform Proposals and the Abandonment of the Family*, 36 Brandeis J. Family L. 241 (1997-98). In the Caribbean countries, where the extended family is culturally important, the laws typically permit the immigration of not only parents, but grandparents. See Leonard Storchevoy, *The Right to Family Reunification in the Immigration Law of the*

Commonwealth Caribbean and the United States: A Comparative Study, 7 Touro Int'l L. Rev. 177, 203-06 (1997).

Page 173, paragraph 4, replace the last sentence with the following:

Until August 1998, the INS granted national interest waivers fairly liberally. See generally Enid Trucios-Haynes, *National Interest Waivers*, July 1995 Immigration Briefings; Wall Street Journal, Aug. 20, 1998, at 1. On August 7, 1998, however, the world of national interest waivers changed dramatically with the decision of the INS Acting Associate Commissioner in *Matter of New York State Dept. of Transportation [NYSDOT]*, I.D. 3363. The decision in *NYSDOT* restricted national interest waivers in several ways. The INS held it is not enough that the applicant has a particular level of training or education. General arguments about the importance of a given field or the urgency of a given issue similarly do not suffice. Nor is it enough to show a shortage of qualified workers in a given field.

Instead, the INS held, an applicant for a national interest waiver must show (1) that the area of employment is one of "substantial intrinsic merit"; (2) that the person's employment will benefit the nation, not just the local area; and (3) that the particular applicant "will serve the national interest to a <u>substantially</u> greater degree than would an available U.S. worker having the same minimum qualifications [emphasis added]." I.D. 3363 at 3-4. To illustrate the second requirement, the INS said "[W]hile education is in the national interest, the impact of a single schoolteacher in one elementary school would not be in the national interest [for waiver purposes]." *Id.* at 3 n.3. For an effective critique of this position, see Stanley Mailman & Stephen Yale-Loehr, *The "National Interest" Waiver*, 4 Bender's Immigration Bulletin 271 (Apr. 1, 1999).

Page 174, subsection b, 2nd paragraph, line 2:

Error: 212(a)(5)(C) should read 212(a)(5)(D).

Page 184, item 5, add a second paragraph:

Professor Nora Demleitner, in a February 8, 1999 letter to the author, added another, highly important dimension. She wrote:

> It seemed to me that many of the issues surrounding labor certification for live-in housekeepers have to do with our perception of women and childcare, women's roles in the household, social class, and society's continued uneasiness about those issues. In addition, the decision [in *Marion Graham*] is also interesting insofar as it is focused

on the issue of U.S. worker replacement without considering, for example, the child's interest. Might it not make more sense (emotionally, if not economically) to leave the child with the caretaker who has been in charge of her since birth?

Page 188, item 13, 3rd-to-last line, at the sentence break, add:

The Labor Department is in the process of replacing the D.O.T. with a computerized database called "O*NET". It will be available on CD-ROM, diskettes, and the Internet. See 75 Interpreter Releases 1622 (Nov. 23, 1998).

Page 197, replace paragraph with the following:

Accepting these and other arguments, the Labor Department in 1998 amended its regulations to allow colleges, universities, and federal research centers to pay researchers the wages prevailing at similar institutions in the area of intended employment. See 63 Fed. Reg. 13756-67 (Mar. 20, 1998), amending 8 C.F.R. § 656.40.

Page 199, 3rd full paragraph, 3d-to-last line, after "see also", insert:

William J. Flynn III & Dilip Patel, *Employers, Employees and Ethics*, in Alfonso Caprara, Rumi Engineer & Barbara Marcouiller (eds.), AILA, Ethics and Your Immigration Practice: Have you Considered . . . ?, at 31-50 (1998).

Page 201, item 6, last line, replace parenthetical with the following:

1147 (1997), expanded and updated in Howard F. Chang, *Migration as International Trade: The Economic Gains from the Liberalized Movement of Labor*, 3 UCLA J. Law & Foreign Affairs 371 (1998).

Page 202, top of page, at end of article citation, add:

The religious workers subcategory, described in INA § 101(a)(27)(C)(ii), has now been extended until September 30, 2000. See Pub. L. 105-54, 111 Stat. 1175 (Oct. 6, 1997).

Page 203, 2nd full paragraph, add at end:

One possibility is that the evasion provision was meant merely to ensure that the investment involves actual risk, rather than a repurchase agreement more in the nature of a loan. On this issue there has been internal disagreement within the INS. See *Matter of Izummi*, I.D. 3360 at 18-25 (INS Assoc. Comm'r for Examinations, July 13, 1998).

Page 204, after 1st paragraph, add:

Investors need not pay the entire minimum amount up front; they need only be "actively in the process of investing" that amount. INA § 203(a)(5)(A)(ii). To meet that requirement, investors have used a variety of methods, including secured promissory notes, balloon payments, options to sell, and pooled investments. Many immigration investment consultants advertised that even a $125,000 investment under certain circumstances could meet the threshold requirement, and the INS in fact approved many such schemes. See Stanley Mailman & Stephen Yale-Loehr, *Controversy over Investor Category*, 3 Bender's Immigration Bulletin 491 (May 15, 1998). The program began to gather steam.

But the bubble burst in December 1997 when the INS General Counsel issued a 36-page legal opinion disapproving many of these arrangements. See Memorandum from the Office of General Counsel to Paul W. Virtue, HQCOU 70/6.1.8 & 70/9-P (Dec. 19, 1997), reproduced in 75 Interpreter Releases No. 9, App. I (Mar. 9, 1998). The opinion also made the change retroactive, resulting in the revocation of previously granted visa petitions. Mailman & Yale-Loehr, above, at 494-95. The INS and the consular officers then proceeded to place 5th preference visa petitions and visa applications on hold. See David Hirson & Catherine I. Mayou, *The Sinking of the Titanic or the Rising of the Phoenix? - An Update on Immigrant Investor Visas*, September 1998 Immigration Briefings.

Page 216, 1st full paragraph, add at end:

For two strong defenses of the family unification program, and corresponding criticisms of the impact of IIRAIRA on family unity, see Lolita Buckner Inniss, *Dutch Uncle Sam: Immigration Reform and Notions of Family*, 36 Brandeis J. Family L. 177 (1997-98); Beth Stickney, *Whither Family Unity? A Post-IIRIRA Update*, December 1998 Immigration Briefings.

Page 216, item 3, line 5, after "workers", insert:

(and now certain others)

Page 219, 1st full paragraph, lines 15-18, replace the Johnson cite with the following:

Berta Esperanza Hernandez-Truyol, *Borders (En)gendered: Normativities, Latinas, and the LatCrit Paradigm*, 72 NYU L. Rev. 882 (1997); Lolita Buckner Innis, *The Legacy of Racially Restrictive Immigration Laws and Policies and the Construction of the American National Identity*, 76 Oreg. L. Rev. 369 (1997) (examining relationships among assimilation, race, and identity in context of immigration policy); Kevin R. Johnson, *"Melting Pot" or "Ring of Fire"?: Assimilation and the Mexican-American Experience*, 85 Cal. L. Rev. 1259 (1997).

Page 219, after 1st full paragraph, add new paragraph:

There are now signs that the political climate is warming. A recent PBS poll suggests that the most virulent anti-immigrant sentiment began to subside at least by the fall of 1997. See U.S.A. Today, Oct. 13, 1997, at 1, 11. From 1993 to 1997, the percentage of respondents who favored reducing or halting immigration dropped from 65% to 46%, largely, one presumes, because of the booming economy. *Id.*

Page 220, 1st full paragraph, add at end:

See also Peter H. Schuck, Citizens, Strangers, and In-Betweens: Essays on Immigration and Citizenship 89-160 (1998); John Scanlan, Book Review, *Something Happened: Descent into the Immigration Maelstrom; or Fear and Loathing in Fortress America*, 4 Indiana J. Global Legal Studies 239 (1996).

Page 220, item 6, replace last sentence with the following:

For a good before-and-after discussion of the work of the Commission, see Carlos Ortiz Miranda, *United States Commission on Immigration Reform: The Interim and Final Reports*, 38 Santa Clara L. Rev. 645 (1998); Carlos O. Miranda, *An Agenda for the Commission on Immigration Reform*, 29 San Diego L. Rev. 701 (1992).

Page 222, before last paragraph, insert the following:

As of February 1999, statutes in some 22 states and many municipal ordinances declare English the "official" language. See William Branigin, *Spread of Spanish Greeted by Some Unwelcome Signs: Businesses Facing Language Restrictions*, Washington Post, Feb. 6, 1999, at A4. The town of Norcross, Georgia, for example, prohibits the posting of commercial signs that are less than 75% English:

> Consider Maria Cobarrubias, who has built her general store into a profitable fixture in the Atlanta suburb of Norcross by catering to a growing Hispanic community that is transforming many parts of the South.
>
> Cobarrubias was stunned to receive a visit recently from the local marshal, who fined her for having a sign with the store's name -- Supermercado Jalisco -- in Spanish. Supermercado is the Spanish word for supermarket, and Jalisco is the Mexican state where Cobarrubias was born. * * *
>
> She said she paid a $115 fine but is thinking about fighting back in court. Enforcement of the ordinance has outraged Mexican diplomats, and the American Civil Liberties Union said it may challenge the law as unconstitutional.
>
> * * *
>
> * * * Officially, the reason is to help police, fire and rescue personnel identify and locate businesses in emergencies. * * *
>
> At a nearby competing grocery called La Mexicana, manager Jaime Elizondo, 42, said he also paid a fine and had to change several words on the store's sign before it opened last spring.
>
> * * *
>
> Sgt. H. Smith, the Norcross marshal, said he has also issued citations to several Korean churches and an "Oriental beauty shop." Some Spanish words are "acceptable," he said, while others, such as "supermercado," must be changed.
>
> "The 'super' is English. But I don't know what 'mercado' means," he said. "If an American was out there driving by, he wouldn't know what that was." * * *
>
> Neighboring Doraville, also home to large numbers of Hispanic and Asian immigrants, has an ordinance like the one in Norcross but has chosen not to enforce it.

Branigan, above. Query: In Norcross and Doraville, is it a crime to post a restaurant sign with the name "Chez Louis"?

As others have shown, the fear that English is losing its dominance seems misplaced. Linguistic assimilation among immigrants and their children is the norm, not the exception. For some useful statistics, see T. Alexander Aleinikoff & Ruben Rumbaut, *Terms of Belonging: Are Models of Membership Self-Fulfilling Prophecies?*, 13 Georgetown Immigration L.J. 1 (1998).

CHAPTER 3

NONIMMIGRANT CATEGORIES

Page 236, last full paragraph, add at end:

In 1997 the INS and the State Department simultaneously issued new regulations that affect eligibility for E-status in several ways. See 8 C.F.R. § 214.2(e); 22 C.F.R. § 41.51; 74 Interpreter Releases 1425 (Sept. 22, 1997). The changes relevant here are reflected below.

Page 237, 1st full paragraph, change the 1st sentence and corresponding citation to read:

Both categories of E-entrants are ordinarily admitted for two years, with an unlimited number of possible two-year extensions. 8 C.F.R. § 214.2(e)(19,20).

Page 237, 1st full paragraph, change the sentence and corresponding citation on lines 6-9 to read:

Both the INS and State Department regulations, however, do require an intent to depart upon termination of E-status. 8 C.F.R. § 214.2(e)(5); 22 C.F.R. §§ 41.51(a)(2) (traders), 41.51(b)(3) (investors).

Page 239, 1st paragraph, replace lines 3-end with the following:

8 C.F.R. § 214.2(e)(14) (investment amount must be "substantial" in relation to total cost of enterprise, sufficient to ensure the investor's financial commitment, and large enough that investor is likely to direct and develop the enterprise). The regulations add that the enterprise may not be "marginal." 8 C.F.R. § 214.2(e)(15).

Page 239, after item 5, add new item 5A:

The treaty trader provision also requires "substantial" trade. For that purpose, the regulations now provide that the arrangement must contemplate ongoing activity, not an isolated transaction. 8 C.F.R. § 214.2(e)(10).

Page 240, 1st paragraph, make two changes:

(1) In lines 4-5, change "the INS has now ruled" to "the INS Benefits Division has taken the position."

(2) At end of paragraph, add the following:

Stanley Mailman, in an October 7, 1998 e-mail to the author, raised the question of how this can practically be done when the U.S. employer must attest that it will pay the prevailing wage. In any event, as Mr. Mailman points out, the INS Associate Commissioner, in whose name the Administrative Appeals Office issues opinions, does not regard previous unpublished INS decisions as binding precedent. See, e.g., *Matter of Izummi*, I.D. 3360 at 14 (INS Assoc. Comm'r for Examinations, July 13, 1998).

Page 242, after 2nd paragraph, add the following:

Since then, however, H1-B admissions have climbed. The fiscal year 1998 cap of 65,000 was reached in May, about eight months into the fiscal year. 75 Interpreter Releases 1472 n.4 (Oct. 26, 1998). After much debate, Congress enacted compromise legislation that raised the numerical ceiling on H1-Bs for three years -- to 115,000 in each of fiscal years 1999 and 2000, and 107,500 in fiscal year 2001. After that, the ceiling reverts permanently to 65,000. See Pub. L. 105-277, 112 Stat. 2681, Div. C, § 411 (Oct. 21, 1998), amending INA § 214(g)(1)(A).

On June 15, 1999, with more than 3 months still remaining in fiscal year 1999, the INS announced that the H-1B applications already granted, when combined with those already filed and likely to be granted, were at or near the new temporary cap of 115,000. 64 Fed. Reg. 32151-53 (June 15, 1999). The INS reported that by then it had processed all applications filed before April 7. As a stopgap measure, it announced it would continue to adjudicate all applications that had already been filed (by the time of the June 15 notice). It would grant all of the applications that were approvable, in the order received, until the cap was reached; the others would also be granted, if approvable, but the work-start date would be no earlier than October 1, 1999, the first day of fiscal year 2000. *Id.* All applications filed after June 15, 1999 would be returned. At the same time, the INS issued proposed regulations to establish a permanent system for dealing with the cap. Under the proposal, which would take effect in fiscal year 2000, the INS would accept and adjudicate all H1-B applications in the order received. Once the cap has been reached, it would then assign the earliest work-start date available. 64 Fed. Reg. 32149-50 (June 15, 1999). Note the cap does not apply to extensions of, or other changes to, existing H1-B aliens.

Page 264, before last paragraph, add new paragraph:

In October 1997 Congress finally made the au pair program permanent. Pub. L. 105-48, 111 Stat. 1165 (Oct. 1, 1997). For an update on the precise requirements, see 74 Interpreter Releases 1546 (Oct. 10, 1997). Today, more than 10,000 families per year make use of the foreign au pair program. *Id.*

Page 265, after 3rd paragraph, add new paragraph:

Effective October 1, 1999 (or possibly earlier), the USIA has been abolished. Its functions have been transferred to the Secretary of State. See Pub. L. 105-277, 112 Stat. 2681, Div. C, §§ 1301, 1311, 1312 (Oct. 21, 1998).

Page 273, line 2, add at end:

[Update: The abolition of the USIA, see above, will require changes to the administrative structure for deciding waiver requests.]

CHAPTER 4

INADMISSIBLE ALIENS

Page 301, 1st full paragraph, add at end:

For an excellent description of the exclusion grounds added or changed by IIRAIRA, see Enid Trucios-Haynes & Lois Gimpel Shaukat, *Grounds of Inadmissibility under the Illegal Immigration Reform and Immigrant Responsibility Act of 1996*, January & February 1998 Immigration Briefings (2 parts); see also DOS Cable, No. 98-State-060539 (Apr. 4, 1998), reproduced in 75 Interpreter Releases at 543-55 (Apr. 20, 1998).

Page 305, replace paragraphs 3 and 4 with the following:

Some of the exclusion grounds encompass aliens who are or were out of status. Another product of IIRAIRA, INA § 212(a)(9)(B), is especially important. It renders certain aliens who have been "unlawfully present" in the United States for 180 days or for one year inadmissible for three years or ten years, respectively. Please read INA § 212(a)(9)(B) carefully at this time.

INA § 212(a)(9)(B)(ii) defines a person as being "unlawfully present" if he or she "is present in the United States after the expiration of the period of stay authorized by the Attorney General or is present in the United States without being admitted or paroled." This definition has generated many difficult issues, some of which the INS has raised and attempted to resolve in a series of internal memoranda.

One important INS position appears in a June 17, 1997 memorandum from then Acting Executive Associate Commissioner Paul Virtue, reproduced in July/August 1997 AILA Monthly Mailing at 635-38. The INS position is that section 212(a)(9)(B) contemplates *continuous* unlawful presence, not an *aggregate* of two or more separate stays. By way of example, it says, a person with two separate four-month periods of unlawful presence would *not* be inadmissible under the 180-day provision. *Id*. Note that the two sub-prongs of section 212(a)(9)(B) are differently worded. The 3-year exclusion refers to unlawful presence for "*a period* of more than 180 days . . . (emphasis added)," while the 10-year exclusion refers simply to unlawful presence "for one year or more". Nonetheless, the INS memo makes clear that its interpretation governs both subprongs.

A subsequent memo from Mr. Virtue, dated September 19, 1997 and reproduced in 2 Bender's Immigration Bulletin at 842-45 (Oct. 15, 1997), furnishes additional guidance, mostly on the question of when presence will be considered "unlawful." The first issue the memo addresses concerns a remedy called "voluntary departure", which you will study in chapter 7. As you will see, it is common for either the INS or an immigration judge to allow a person under certain circumstances to depart voluntarily rather than be formally removed. Typically the person is given until a certain date to leave. The INS memo, reversing an earlier interpretation, holds that an alien who is granted the remedy of "voluntary departure" is not considered "unlawfully present" until the due date for his or her departure. *Id.* at 842-43.

What happens if a nonimmigrant violates the terms of his or her admittance (other than by overstaying)? Suppose, for example, a person admitted as an F-1 student drops out of school or works without authorization. Does his or her presence become "unlawful" at that point? The violation of the terms of admission makes the person deportable, INA § 237(a)(1)(C)(i), but the memo takes the position that the *presence* does not thereby become unlawful, and thus the 180-day and one-year periods do not start to run, until the immigration judge hears the case and determines that the violation has occurred. 2 Bender's Immigration Bulletin at 843-44.

There has been little controversy on those issues. In contrast, there has been major controversy on another, immensely important issue. When the INS believes someone is deportable, it begins removal proceedings by filing a document called a "notice to appear." INA § 239(a)(1). Because of huge administrative backlogs, it can take months or sometimes even years to hold the removal hearing, and there is no authority to remove the alien before the hearing has been held. Does the time from the notice to appear until the issuance of a removal order count as unlawful presence? The INS memo says yes, unless the alien ultimately is found not to be deportable. 2 Bender's Immigration Bulletin at 844. (Further complications arise if the immigration judge finds the person deportable but grants any of several discretionary remedies that you will study in chapter 7.)

But that is not necessarily the end of the story. The Executive Office for Immigration Review (which, you will recall, houses the immigration judges and the Board of Immigration Appeals, among others) apparently disagrees with the INS interpretation. It believes that time spent in removal proceedings is not unlawful presence. This disagreement is said to be one of the reasons that as of this writing the Department of Justice has yet to issue final regulations implementing the "unlawful presence" provision. May 1999 AILA Monthly Mailing at 455. For a highly useful discussion, see Stephen Yale-Loehr, *Beating the Bar: Avoiding, Delaying or Remedying Unlawful Presence*, 3 Bender's Immigration Bulletin 779 (Aug. 1, 1998).

The last category of immigration-control-related exclusion grounds concerns the removal process more directly. INA § 212(a)(6)(B) renders inadmissible for five years any alien who, without reasonable cause, fails to attend his or her removal hearing. Under INA § 212(a)(9)(A), aliens who are ordered removed are generally inadmissible for either 5 years or 10 years, depending on whether they were removed upon or after arrival (20 years for second offenders, forever for "aggravated felons", a term that you will examine later). The Attorney General may waive section 9(A).

Finally, an alien who was unlawfully present for "an aggregate period of more than one year" or who was removed for any reason, and who then enters or attempts to enter "without being admitted," becomes inadmissible for at least ten years, after which time the Attorney General may grant permission to reapply for admission. INA § 212(a)(9)(C). Since the statute expressly uses the term "aggregate", the INS position is that two or more separate periods may be aggregated for purposes of section 212(a)(9)(C). See Virtue memo of Sept. 19, 1997, in 2 Bender's Immigration Bulletin at 636, 637 (contrasting this interpretation with that of the slightly different language in section 212(a)(9)(B)).

Page 306, Problem 2, change the following dates:

1. In line 8, change "November 1" to "May 1."

2. In line 9, change "November 1, 2004" to "May 1, 2001."

Page 308, 1st paragraph, add at end:

See also the new exclusion ground for foreign government officials who, within the preceding two years, were responsible for "particularly severe violations of religious freedom". INA § 212(a)(2)(G), added by International Religious Freedom Act of 1998, Pub. L. 105-292, 112 Stat. 2787, 2814, § 604 (Oct. 27, 1998). The same provision excludes their spouses and children.

Page 314, Problem 3, line 2:

Change "his daughter" to "his 30-year-old daughter."

Page 314, section C, introductory paragraph, replace the last sentence with the following two paragraphs:

As you will see in chapter 6, one *deportability* ground is that the person has been convicted of an "aggravated felony", now defined expansively to cover a wide range of criminal offenses. (There is no analogous *inadmissibility* ground.) You might have noticed that relief under INA § 212(h) is unavailable to anyone who has been convicted of an aggravated felony after having been admitted as a lawful permanent resident. In *Matter of Michel*, I.D. 3335 (BIA, Jan. 30, 1998), the Board interpreted this disqualification literally, holding it did not bar 212(h) relief to an otherwise eligible aggravated felon who had never been admitted to permanent residence. Despite the anomaly of treating former permanent residents more harshly than those otherwise similarly situated, the Board felt bound by the plain language.

The same portion of section 212(h) also disqualifies anyone who has previously been admitted as a lawful permanent resident and who, since that admission, has not lawfully resided continuously in the United States for at least seven years "immediately preceding the initiation of [removal] proceedings." (Keep this language in mind when you do Problem 4 below.) This strange provision was interpreted in *Matter of Ayala-Arevalo*, I.D. 3371 (Nov. 30, 1998). Ayala was admitted as a permanent resident and did not subsequently reside in the United States for seven years. At the time of his admission, he in fact had been inadmissible (on fraud grounds). He thus argued that he had not been "lawfully" admitted for permanent residence and therefore did not fall within the disqualification. The BIA disagreed. To avoid an "arbitrary and capricious" result, *id.* at 4-5, it interpreted the disqualification as covering even aliens who had been "unlawfully" admitted to permanent residence. The decision prompted a strong dissent from Board member Lory Rosenberg. *Id.* at 6-11. Contrast the statutory interpretation approach in *Ayala-Arevalo* with that in *Michel*, where the Board had construed the statute literally even in the face of an anomaly.

Page 317, replace the 2nd, 3rd, and 4th full paragraphs (i.e., "Most importantly, . . ." to "execute a binding affidavit") with the following:

INS interim regulations spell out most of the details. 62 Fed. Reg. 54,346-56 (Oct. 20, 1997), adding 8 C.F.R. § 213a; see also INS, Fact Sheet (Oct. 20, 1997), reproduced in 2 Bender's Immigration Bulletin at 896 (Nov. 1, 1997) (elaborating on the interim regulations and the affidavit of support form); Beth Stickney, *Whither Family Unity? A Post-IIRIRA Update*, December 1998 Immigration Briefings; Charles Wheeler, *Affidavit of Support: A Year in Review*, 4 Bender's Immigration Bulletin at 97 (Feb. 1, 1999); Charles Wheeler, *The Affidavit of Support and Sponsorship Requirements: A Critical Analysis*, June 1998 Immigration Briefings. For reproductions of the INS standardized form affidavit of support and accompanying instructions, see U.S. Dept. of State, Visa Bulletin (Dec. 1997)(inserted after page 4); T. Alexander Aleinikoff, David A. Martin & Hiroshi Motomura (eds.), Immigration and Nationality Laws of the United States (paperback supplement published annually, section entitled "Selected Immigration Forms").

The most important change is that the affidavit is now a binding contract. It must be "legally enforceable against the sponsor by the sponsored alien, the Federal Government, any state (or any political subdivision of such state), or by any other entity that provides any means-tested public benefit." INA § 213A(a)(1)(B). The promise is binding for 40 qualifying quarter-years after the alien last receives benefits or until naturalization if sooner. INA § 213A(a)(2).

The sponsor must be a United States national or a lawful permanent resident alien, over age 18, and domiciled in the United States. INA § 213A(f)(1)(A,B,C). The sponsor must be the person who is petitioning for the alien's admission. INA § 213A(f)(1)(D). If the petitioner lacks the required resources (see below), he or she may join with another person to co-sponsor the alien. INA § 213A(f)(5).

The combination of the foregoing requirements has significant effects independent of the public charge issue. Before IIRAIRA, a United States citizen could petition for the admission of an otherwise qualifying alien family member even if the petitioner was living overseas. That is no longer possible. Since the petitioner must be a sponsor (either alone or jointly), and since a sponsor has to be domiciled in the United States, citizens domiciled overseas may no longer petition for the admission of their family members. See David A. Martin, (then) General Counsel, INS, Legal Opinion 97-10 (July 8, 1997), reproduced in 75 Interpreter Releases at 380-83 (Mar. 16, 1998). Nor, according to the INS, can a citizen domiciled overseas solve the problem by enlisting a co-sponsor domiciled in the United States; a co-sponsor will not suffice unless the petitioner is also eligible to be a sponsor. *Id.* The only opening in such cases is that the citizen petitioner, although physically overseas, might be able to prove that his or her foreign presence is temporary and that the plan is to return to the United States. *Id.*

Page 317, last full paragraph, line 1:

Change "Second, the" to "The".

Page 318, 3rd full paragraph:

(1) In line 1, change 1996 to 1999.

(2) Substitute the following dollar amounts:

1	$ 8,240
2	11,060
3	13,880
4	16,700
5	19,520
6	22,340
7	25,160
8	27,980

Page 318, replace footnote 14 with the following:

14. See 64 Fed. Reg. 13428-30 (Mar. 18, 1999). Higher figures apply to Hawaii, and still higher figures apply to Alaska. *Id.* at 13428-29. NB: Sponsors' incomes must be 125% of the income levels shown in this chart.

Page 319, after item 6, add new item 7:

7. For some insightful observations concerning the "chilling" effects of the 1996 reforms on immigrants in need of welfare, see Linton Joaquin & Braden Cancilla, *Protecting Immigrants and the Community: A New Approach to Public Charge Determinations*, 76 Interpreter Releases No. 22 (June 7, 1999).

Page 320, after 1st full paragraph, add new paragraph:

Tuberculosis, another communicable disease that renders aliens inadmissible, has recently prompted renewed concern. See Kimberly A. Johns & Christos Varkoutas, *The Tuberculosis Crisis: The Deadly Consequence of Immigration Policies and Welfare Reform*, 15 J. Contemporary Health L. & Policy 101 (1998).

CHAPTER 5

ADMISSION PROCEDURE

Page 328, 4th paragraph, add at end:

See generally Commission on Immigration Reform, Becoming an American: Immigration and Immigrant Policy 161-69 (recommending consolidation of all admission functions in State Department), 175-83 (recommending establishment of independent agency to review immigration-related administrative decisions) (Sept. 1997).

Page 329, 2nd full paragraph, delete the reference in the last sentence to various INA subsections, and add at end:

Linda Kelly, *Stories from the Front: Seeking Refuge for Battered Immigrants in the Violence against Women Act*, 92 Northwestern L. Rev. 665 (1998).

Please read INA §§ 204(a)(1)(A)(iii,iv), 204(a)(1)(B)(ii,iii). Then read the following fact situation, and try to answer the accompanying questions, drafted by Professor Linda Kelly:

Linda Kelly, The Violence Against Women Act: An Overview
[unpublished paper reprinted with permission]

Sonya's Story:

We met at a vocational and technical education school. We began dating and fell in love. I was four months into my pregnancy when we got married. The abuse started when I became pregnant and gradually progressed in severity. The verbal insults turned into physical abuse. When I fought back he would beat me and then force me to have sex with him. He told me that because I was not willing to please him as a good wife should, I had become a mere servant in his home. He would hide food. He said that I could eat it off the floor since I was no more than a dog. When he hid my passport I hid one of his guns that he would keep on top of the television. The police only told him to be careful with Latin women because they had fiery tempers. He laughed as they left and told me that would show me that he had the power because he was American and that no one would believe me. He would yell at me that I was nothing but an immigrant and that he, as a citizen, had all the power.

Question 1. What problems may a victim of domestic violence like Sonya encounter in documenting and proving the abuse? How does a domestic violence survivor's position as an undocumented immigrant compound this problem?

Question 2. What problems may a victim of domestic violence encounter in documenting and proving good faith marriage? How does a domestic violence survivor's position as an undocumented immigrant compound this problem?

* * *

Page 334, before Problem set, insert new item 8:

8. In addition to criminal and civil legislation and to the ethical constraints imposed by state disciplinary codes, attorneys (and others) who practice before the INS or the EOIR are subject to the Justice Department's own disciplinary rules. For the moment, those rules can be found in 8 C.F.R. § 292. The Justice Department, however, has issued proposed regulations that would alter both the substantive grounds and procedures for disciplining practitioners in immigration proceedings. See 63 Fed. Reg. 2901 (Jan. 20, 1998). These are taken up on pages 552-57 below and in the corresponding passages in this Supplement.

Page 336, footnote 6, add at end:

The visa waiver pilot program has now been extended to April 30, 2000. See Pub. L. 105-173, 112 Stat. 56 (Apr. 27, 1998). Previous interim regulations adding new countries to the list have now been finalized. 63 Fed. Reg. 71726-27 (Dec. 30, 1998), amending 8 C.F.R. § 217.

Page 340, before the triple asterisk, add the following:

4. As a practical matter, consular officers exercise a great deal of subjective discretion. See Michael Maggio, Larry S. Rifkin & Sheila T. Starkey, *Immigration Fundamentals for International Lawyers*, 13 Amer. Univ. Int'l L. Rev. 857, 868-71 (1998).

A recent scandal at the United States consulate in Sao Paulo, Brazil exposed the dangers of those powers. The consulate engaged in explicit racial and economic stereotyping and fired an officer who refused to comply with the "profiles". The officer sued and won a reversal. See *Olsen v. Albright*, 990 F. Supp. 31 (D.D.C. 1997).

According to the manual issued by the consulate, "Officers sometimes use abbreviations on the [visa application forms]: RK = Rich Kid, LP= Looks Poor, TP = Talks Poor, LR = Looks Rough, TC = Take Care." Some of the stated reasons for denying nonimmigrant visas included "Slimy looking[;] wears jacket on shoulders w/ earring", "bad appearance", "looks + talks poor." 990 F. Supp. at 33. The manual also contained a passage headed "KOREAN/CHINESE FRAUD", which said "Major fraud; hard to check. * * * Visas are rarely issued to these groups unless they have had previous visas and are older." *Id.* The manual then listed certain Brazilian cities "known for fraud" -- most of them with predominantly black populations -- and cautioned that "anyone born in these locations is suspect unless older, well-traveled, etc." *Id.* A separate memorandum distributed to all the U.S. consulates in Brazil instructed that "Arab and Chinese last names set off bells and whistles, regardless of what passport/nationality they may have. * * * Most Brazilians have no interest in [assuming a false identity], but Arabs and Chinese are two groups to worry about." *Id.* at 34.

Apart from the economic and racial stereotyping, the dismissed officer's superiors had told him "that he should spend approximately three minutes per interview *and that he should attempt to achieve a thirty percent refusal rate.* To achieve these goals, they said, Plaintiff should base his judgment on the profiles" [emphasis added]. *Id.*

As the court noted, *id.* at 37, the law is otherwise: "[N]o person shall receive any preference or priority or be discriminated against in the issuance of an immigrant visa because of the person's race, sex, nationality, place of birth, or place of residence [except as specifically provided by the INA]." INA § 202(a)(1)(A).

Page 341, 2nd full paragraph, add at end:

See also Commission on Immigration Reform, Becoming an American: Immigration and Immigrant Policy at 175-83 (Sept. 1997) (advocating administrative review of selected visa denials, as well as judicial review, *id.* at 82).

Page 345, paragraph below long dash, line 5, after Kennedy citation, add:

H.R. 1156 (1999) (per Rep. Frank).

Page 354, after item 4, add a new item 4A:

4A. How does the explicit racial profiling and other improper criteria employed in Sao Paulo [see item 4 above], together with at least the possibility of more subtle practices in other United States consulates, affect the present issue? Are these practices an argument for or against review of visa denials?

Page 356, after last full paragraph, add new paragraph:

At a typical airport, seaport, or land border, travelers present their papers to immigration inspectors who perform "primary inspection" -- for most people, a quick process that entails scanning the passport (and visa, if there is one) and possibly checking a "lookout" list on the computer. If there are doubts or complications, the person is referred to a "secondary inspections" area for more intensive scrutiny. See Daniel C. Horne & L. Ari Weitzhandler, *Asylum Law after the Illegal Immigration Reform and Immigrant Responsibility Act*, April 1997 Immigration Briefings at 13.

Page 363, 1st paragraph of subsection 3, replace last sentence with the following:

You will see a more detailed description of general BIA procedure on pages 542-43 below. The BIA in certain cases employs a more summary procedure, which is discussed on pages 708-11 below and updated in this Supplement (see passage adding new item 12 to page 711).

Page 365, replace last full paragraph with the following:

As of January 1999, the INS was averaging about 1200 expedited removals per week. Patrick J. McDonnell, *Deportations Increase Almost 50% in U.S.*, Los Angeles Times, Jan. 9, 1999. Most of the debate has concerned the modified version of expedited removal reserved for asylum claims, a subject to which we return in chapter 9. On that front, there are some early indications of disturbing problems, but, because the INS has denied most requests for observation, verification has been difficult. See generally Karen Musalo, Deborah Anker & J. Edward Taylor, *The Expedited Removal Study: Report on the First Year of Implementation*, 75 Interpreter Releases 973 (July 17, 1998), as well as pages 916-17 below and the corresponding passages in this Supplement.

Page 367, replace the 2nd, 3rd, and 4th full paragraphs with the following:

All those restrictions (and some new ones) were at least temporarily softened in August 1994, when Congress enacted temporary legislation designed to permit and even encourage adjustment of status. Section 506(b) of Pub. L. 103-317, 108 Stat. 1724, 1765-66 (Aug. 26, 1994), added a new subsection 245(i) to the INA. This amendment exempted certain aliens from the ineligibilities created by their entries without inspection or by subsection 245(c). To qualify for a 245(i) exemption, however, the alien had to pay an additional penalty fee of $1000. Former INA § 245(i)(1). (Children under 17 and certain spouses and unmarried children of legalized aliens were excused from the penalty fee.) Congress passed this provision both to raise revenue and to encourage applicants for permanent residence to use adjustment of status rather than overburden U.S. consulates abroad.

These temporary provisions survived until January 14, 1998. Except for visa petitions or labor certification applications filed before that date, section 245(i) is no longer in force. Pub. L. 105-119, § 111(a), 111 Stat. 2440, 2458 (Nov. 26, 1997), amending INA § 245(i).

At the same time, Congress added a partly analogous provision solely for certain employment-based applicants. Under INA § 245(k), otherwise eligible applicants for the 1st, 2nd, 3rd, and some 4th preference employment-based slots could adjust their status, even if currently or formerly out of status, provided they entered lawfully and were not out of status more than 180 days.

One of the reasons the former version of section 245(i) was so important was its interaction with another provision that you studied in chapter 4. INA § 212(a)(9)(B)(i)(I), you will recall, renders inadmissible for three years any alien who has been unlawfully present more than 180 days but less than one year. Importantly, though, the inadmissibility attaches only upon the person's departure from the United States before the commencement of removal proceedings. Thus, if a person who has been out of status more than 180 days but who now meets all the substantive requirements for immigrant status leaves the United States to obtain his or her visa, the person becomes inadmissible, and therefore ineligible for a visa, for three years. The same point applies to section 212(a)(9)(B)(i)(II), the one-year unlawful presence/ ten-year bar. In contrast, if the person were allowed to apply for adjustment of status, he or she would not have to leave the country and thus would not be inadmissible, even though out of status. For aliens in this situation, therefore, there was much more at stake than the expense and inconvenience of traveling overseas to get the visa. The person's very ability to become a lawful permanent resident in the near future hinged on section 245(i).

At this time, please read INA § 245(a,b,c, and k).

Page 368, delete item 3.

Page 369, after the heading "Problems", insert the following:

To do the Problems that follow, you will need to consult INA § 245(a,c, and k) and review sections 212(a)(6)(A), 212(a)(9)(A), and 212(a)(9)(B). In each Problem, assume the present date is after January 14, 1998.

Page 369, Problem 2, change to read as follows:

Alien Y entered the United States without inspection or admission 15 months ago. Now married to a United States citizen, he would like to become a lawful permanent resident. Will he be able to obtain either an immigrant visa at a U.S. consulate overseas or adjustment of status in the United States?

Page 369, Problem 3, make two changes:

(1) In line 6, after the word "mother", add "living in the United States."

(2) In line 7, after the word "which", add "you should assume".

Page 369, Problem 4, change to read as follows:

W, a citizen of Pakistan, entered the United States on a student visa and was admitted for the duration of his student status. He enrolled at Arizona State University to do a bachelor's degree in physics. In the fall of his junior year, a large manufacturing company offered him a permanent position that was to begin immediately after graduation. W, delighted, consulted you, an immigration lawyer, as soon as he received the offer. You helped the company apply for and receive labor certification, and in March of his junior year the INS approved the required visa petition. His priority date became current in January of his senior year. You immediately filed an application for adjustment of status. On May 15, while the application was still pending, W graduated. On July 1, to your surprise, the INS denied adjustment on the ground that W had once been convicted, in Pakistan, of a crime involving moral turpitude. Your research found no case precisely on point, but analogous cases suggested the INS was probably wrong to classify the particular crime as one that involves moral turpitude. You informally reported your findings to the District Director of the local INS office, but you could not convince her. On July 15, W's F-1 status expired. It is now August 1. The INS has not instituted any removal proceedings. W has not worked, and within a few months his savings will run out. What are your options?

CHAPTER 6

DEPORTABLE ALIENS

Page 389, footnote c, line 3:

Change "10-13" to "10-14."

Page 396, line 3:

Again change "10-13" to "10-14."

Page 399, after 2nd paragraph, add new paragraph:

In *Matter of Collado-Munoz*, I.D. 3333 (BIA, Feb. 26, 1998) (amended opinion), the Board held that a returning resident who falls within one of the six subcategories listed in section 101(a)(13)(C) is to be regarded as seeking admission. In such circumstances, the Board held, *Fleuti* is irrelevant. The Board did not acknowledge any of the arguments made above. In contrast, the dissent of Board member Lory Rosenberg made the same point suggested above -- that the word "unless" ordinarily does not imply the converse. She gave additional examples, drawn mostly from other legal settings, to illustrate the point. *Id.* at 9-23. Later the same year a federal district court reached the conclusion implied here and then expressly urged by member Rosenberg: Returning residents who do not fit any of the six subcategories are not regarded as seeking admission; for those returning residents who fall within any of the six subcategories, the court applies the *Fleuti* doctrine to determine whether the departure meaningfully interrupted the person's permanent residence in the United States. *Richardson v. Reno*, 994 F. Supp. 1466 (S.D.N.Y. 1998), rev'd on other grounds, 162 F.3d 1338 (11th Cir. 1998) (amended opinion). Thus, whether an implied converse should be read into the statute, and the current status of *Fleuti*, are still open questions.

Page 399, 3rd full paragraph, add before last sentence:

The Board in *Collado-Munoz* did not explain how the word "entry," in the "admission" definition of section 101(a)(13), is to be defined.

Page 400, line 2, add at end:

Consider also section 101(a)(13)(C)(iii), which covers the person who "has engaged in illegal activity after having departed the United States." On its face this language is even broader than subsection C(v).

Page 405, before last paragraph, add new paragraph:

False citizenship claims actually raise one other interesting issue, which Professor Gerald Neuman noted in an October 23, 1997 e-mail to the author. In *Reid v. INS*, 420 U.S. 619 (1975), decided before IIRAIRA, the Supreme Court held that an alien who gains entry by falsely claiming to be a United States citizen has not been "inspected" and therefore is deportable for having entered without inspection. As noted earlier, IIRAIRA eliminated entry without inspection from the list of deportability grounds but added presence without admission to the list of inadmissibility grounds. The question raised by Professor Neuman is whether *Reid* survives IIRAIRA. If entry via a false citizenship claim still results in no "inspection", then the alien presumably has also not been "admitted", because the latter requires a lawful entry "after inspection." INA § 101(a)(13)(A). (Actually there is probably no "lawful" entry in any event.) Under that interpretation, an alien who gains entry by falsely claiming United States citizenship is inadmissible for being present without admission.

Page 410, after 4th full paragraph, add new paragraph:

Despite the increased congressional attention, the logistical barriers to removing high proportions of criminal aliens remain formidable. See generally Peter H. Schuck & John Williams, *Removing Criminal Aliens: The Pitfalls and Promises of Federalism*, 22 Harv. J. L. & Public Policy 367 (1999) (lamenting the slow pace of removal of criminal aliens, ascribing some of the obstacles to federalism, and urging greater use of state law enforcement personnel).

Page 415, item 4, add at end:

But see the discussion of *Matter of Roldan*, I.D. 3377 (BIA, Mar. 3, 1999), in this Supplement, corresponding to casebook pages 431-32.

Page 428, 1st paragraph of item 5, add at end:

See Franco Capriotti, Linda Friedman Ramirez, Leslie Norikay & Rachel Unger, *Small-Time Crime, Big-Time Trouble: The New Immigration Laws*, 13 Crim. Justice # 2 (1998) (cautioning criminal defense lawyers that, if the client is an alien, even a seemingly minor crime can jeopardize his or her immigration status); Susan L. Pilcher, *Justice without a Blindfold: Criminal Proceedings and the Alien Defendant*, 50 Arkansas L. Rev. 269, 328-32 (1997) (taking a broad view of the responsibilities of both defense counsel and prosecutor).

Page 430, last full paragraph, add at end:

For a strong defense of the latter view, see Victor C. Romero, *Expanding the Circle of Membership by Reconstructing the "Alien": Lessons from Social Psychology and the "Promise Enforcement" Cases*, 32 Univ. Mich. Journal of Law Reform 1, 20-34 (1998).

Pages 431-32, replace all of subsection (ii) with the following:

ii. Expungements

Under various federal and state statutes, it is sometimes possible to expunge criminal convictions. The statutes are quite diverse: Some apply to youth offenders, others to first offenders, and still others to adults who have been sentenced to probation. Precisely when such expungements will erase the convictions for immigration purposes has been a difficult question. A long line of cases has fashioned complex rules that hinge on whether the statute is state or federal, whether it is for adults or youth offenders, and whether the conviction is a crime involving moral turpitude, a drug offense, a firearms offense, or some other crime.

Much of the case law developed before 1996. In that year, Congress added to the INA a specific definition of "conviction." INA § 101(a)(48)(A). The definition for the most part tracked the language of the then most recent BIA decisions. In a dramatic shift, the BIA in 1999 interpreted the statutory language to mean that expungement under a state rehabilitative statute never erases the conviction for immigration purposes. *Matter of Roldan*, I.D. 3377 (BIA, Mar. 3, 1999). The Board based its decision on what it believed to be the plain language of the statute and on the congressional purpose of promoting uniform results from state to state. There were two strong dissents.

At least two uncertainties remain. The Board addressed only the issue of expungements under *state* law; it expressly left open whether expungements under the *federal* First Offender Act, 18 U.S.C. § 3607, still eliminate convictions for immigration purposes. The statutory definition of conviction makes no explicit distinction between state and federal convictions, but the issue is how to interpret the First Offender Act.

It is not yet known how the courts will react to *Roldan* if presented with the same issue. As you have seen throughout this course, the courts frequently defer to the interpretations placed on federal statutes by the administrative agencies charged with implementing them. In any event, the opportunity for the courts to express their views might never arise. As you will see in chapter 8, Congress in IIRAIRA purported to bar judicial review of the vast majority of crime-related removal orders. INA § 242(a)(2)(C). As you will also see, however, some courts have found either statutory or constitutional means to review on the merits. In addition, some crime-related removal orders -- including, usually, those based on crimes involving moral turpitude -- are still judicially reviewable even under the most literal reading of the statute. Thus, the possibility of judicial departures from *Roldan* cannot be dismissed.

Consider the following two questions:

1. As a policy matter, should expungements erase *any* criminal convictions, for purposes of deportability?

2. How do the philosophical premises for recognizing at least certain expungements compare with the philosophical premises that underlie the definition of "conviction" in INA § 101(a)(48)(A)?

Page 443, subsection (d), lines 2 and 4:

In both lines, substitute "admission" for "entry."

Page 447, after citation to "18 U.S.C. § 16", add the following:

In *Xiong v. INS*, 173 F.3d 601 (7th Cir. 1999), the court held that, to determine whether an offense falls within prong (b) of the above definition, one considers the language of the statute and, if the statute covers both crimes that involve violence and crimes that don't, the charging papers. The court went on to hold that statutory rape is not a crime of violence unless the victim is particularly young or the age difference particularly great. Consensual intercourse between an 18-year-old defendant and his 15-year-old girlfriend was held not to be a crime of violence. *Id.* at 604-07. In contrast, driving under the influence has been held to be a crime of violence, under prong (b) above. *Matter of Magallanes-Garcia*, I.D. 3341 (BIA, Mar. 19, 1998) (amended opinion).

Page 448, 1st full paragraph, add at end:

Under this expanded definition, even petit larceny has been held to be an aggravated felony. *United States v. Graham*, 169 F.3d 787 (3rd Cir. 1999). In *Graham*, the court also held that for immigration purposes a misdemeanor can be an aggravated felony.

Page 449, after 2nd full paragraph, add the following:

For present purposes it is enough to note these issues rather than try to resolve them. See generally *Matter of Lettman*, I.D. 3370 (BIA, Nov. 5, 1998). The complexity has prompted two commentators to say, in reference to the retroactivity issue, "If you're not confused, you don't understand the situation." James P. Fleissner & James A. Shapiro, *Federal Sentences for Aliens Convicted of Illegal Reentry Following Deportation: Who Needs the Aggravation?*, 9 Georgetown Immigration L.J. 451 (1995).

Page 462, 1st paragraph, add at end:

For an argument that retroactive deportation violates due process, see Nancy Morawetz, *Rethinking Retroactive Deportation Laws and the Due Process Clause*, 73 NYU L. Rev. 97 (1998).

CHAPTER 7

RELIEF FOR DEPORTABLE ALIENS

Page 465, footnote 1, insert before the first sentence:

Professor Elwin Griffith, in *The Road between the Section 212(c) Waiver and Cancellation of Removal under Section 240A of the Immigration and Nationality Act -- The Impact of the 1996 Reform Legislation*, 12 Georgetown Immigration L.J. 65 (1997), comprehensively analyzes the issues that arose under former INA § 212(c) and the effect of substituting cancellation of removal.

Page 467, last paragraph, line 2, at the sentence break add a new sentence:

Hernandez was deportable for having entered without inspection, a charge for which there was no analogous exclusion ground.

Page 472, after 1st paragraph, add a new paragraph:

The 1996 changes have also generated some complex issues concerning retroactivity. Reversing the BIA, the Attorney General held in *Matter of Soriano*, I.D. 3289, 1996 Westlaw 426888 (A.G., Feb. 21, 1997), that the new restrictions apply even to aliens whose deportation proceedings had already begun before the enactment of the changes. Several courts of appeals have rejected that view, holding the changes to be prospective only. See, e.g., *Mayers v. INS*, No. 97-5537 (11th Cir., May 20, 1999); *Sandoval v. Reno*, 166 F.3d 225 (3rd Cir. 1999); *Henderson v. INS*, 157 F.3d 106 (2d Cir. 1998); *Goncalves v. Reno*, 144 F.3d 110 (1st Cir. 1998). In those circuits, the Justice Department will not apply the new restrictions retroactively. In others, retroactivity will be the rule. An April 30, 1999 amicus letter from 44 full-time law professors who teach immigration, drafted by Prof. Hiroshi Motomura, urges the Attorney General to reconsider *Soriano* in the light of these and other developments.

Page 472, subsection 5, 1st paragraph, add at end:

The BIA in 1978 summarized the common positive and negative factors that would guide the discretionary determination under then INA § 212(c). See *Matter of Marin*, 16 I. & N. Dec. 581, 584-85 (BIA, 1978). These same factors continue to govern discretion under cancellation of removal part A. *Matter of C.V.T.*, I.D. 3342 (BIA, Feb. 12, 1998).

Page 473, Problem 2, lines 4-5:

Delete the parenthetical sentence.

Page 474, line 1:

Change "240(b)" to "240A(b)".

Page 474, last paragraph and page 475, 1st paragraph, delete both and replace them with the following:

Finally, note that under INA § 240A(e)(1) "the Attorney General may not cancel the removal and adjust the status under this section" (or under the former suspension of deportation provision) of more than 4000 aliens in any fiscal year. As this language indicates, this remedy accomplishes two things: It avoids removal, and it results in permanent resident status. Does the quoted language permit the Attorney General to cancel the removals of more than 4000 aliens in a given fiscal year as long as she doesn't *both* cancel removal and adjust status for more than 4000? Or did Congress consider the two parts inseparable, so that the 4000 cap applies independently to each of the two actions? One court, in an action brought by aliens who had lost out because of the cap, found the legal issue close enough to warrant affirming a preliminary injunction. See *Barahona-Gomez v. Reno*, 167 F.3d 1228 (9th Cir. 1999).

The Justice Department's interim regulations regard the two parts of the remedy as inseparable and establish a queuing system analogous to the preference-based quota systems that you saw in chapter 2. Once relief has been granted to 4000 applicants in a given fiscal year, immigration judges and the BIA may not grant relief in any further cases that year, even conditionally. They may deny pending applications for cancellation on certain statutory eligibility grounds but will reserve decision on all other pending applications. These pending applications will be taken up in the order in which they were filed, as soon as the quota permits. See 63 Fed. Reg. 52134, 52140 (Sept. 30, 1998), adding 8 C.F.R. § 240.21(c)(1); see generally Nadine Wettstein, *The Peddler Sells His Caps: The EOIR and INS Issue a New Rule on the Suspension/Cancellation Ceiling*, 3 Bender's Immigration Bulletin 1083 (Nov. 1, 1998). While the applications are pending, the person will remain "in proceedings" and will not "normally" be removed. 63 Fed. Reg. at 52137.

The Nicaraguan Adjustment and Central American Relief Act, Pub. L. 105-100, Title II, 111 Stat. 2160, 2193 (Nov. 19, 1997) [NACARA], among other things relaxed the substantive criteria for cancellation of removal part B for certain nationals of Guatemala, El Salvador, the Soviet Union and its successor republics, and most Eastern European nations. The details are discussed in subsection (iv) below. For now, it is enough to note that these NACARA adjustments are not counted against the 4000 limit. INA § 240A(e)(3)(A). Cancellation applicants whose deportation proceedings were pending on April 1, 1997, and who applied under the special suspension of deportation provision for battered spouses and children, are also exempt from the 4000 cap. INA § 240A(e)(3)(B).

Page 478, replace last two paragraphs with the following:

The issue of when hardship is "extreme" (now "exceptional and extremely unusual") can surface in either of two distinct settings that it is crucial to separate. The issue arises in its most direct form when an alien in removal proceedings applies to the immigration judge for cancellation. The applicant has the burden of establishing the required hardship (along with all the other elements of removal). Since the immigration judge's decision whether to order an alien removed is appealable to the BIA, the BIA frequently becomes enmeshed in hardship determinations as well. Before IIRAIRA, when the courts could freely review denials of suspension of deportation, they too would have frequent occasion to contribute to the law on extreme hardship.

IIRAIRA § 306(a)(2) has at least curbed judicial involvement in these issues. It bars the courts from reviewing "any judgment regarding the granting of relief under section . . . 240A." INA § 242(a)(2)(B)(i). As you will see in chapter 8, it is still not clear whether that provision eliminates all judicial review of denials of cancellation.

Page 479, last paragraph, line 7:

Change "a BIA decision either denying reopening or denying cancellation is reviewable in the court of appeals" to "a BIA decision denying reopening, and possibly a BIA decision denying cancellation on certain grounds, are reviewable in the courts of appeals."

Page 480, footnote 5, add at end:

Sarmadi v. INS, 121 F.3d 1319, 1322 (9th Cir. 1997); *King Sang Chow v. INS*, 113 F.3d 659, 664 (7th Cir. 1997).

Page 498, after 1st paragraph, add a new subsection:

iv. NACARA

As a result of prolonged civil war in Nicaragua, Guatemala and El Salvador and some related legal and political developments in the United States, there are hundreds of thousands of undocumented Central Americans who have lived in uncertain status in the United States for many years. You will see more on this subject in chapter 9, in the context of asylum and related remedies.

In an attempt to alleviate at least part of the problem, Congress in 1997 passed the Nicaraguan Adjustment and Central American Relief Act, Pub. L. 105-100, Title II, 111 Stat. 2160, 2193 (Nov. 19, 1997), best known as NACARA. This statute granted special dispensations to nationals of certain named countries. The relief it provided is of two kinds.

The more generous relief, in the nature of an amnesty, is for certain nationals of Nicaragua and Cuba. It is discussed in the subsection on legalization, below. (A subsequent, more limited amnesty for certain Haitian nationals is simultaneously discussed.)

Certain nationals of selected other countries --Guatemala, El Salvador, the former USSR and its successor republics, and most Eastern European nations -- received a lesser but still important form of relief that will be taken up here. They received the right to apply for cancellation of removal (and adjustment of status) under the less onerous substantive criteria embodied in the pre-IIRAIRA suspension of deportation provision. This latter relief is usually referred to as "special rule" cancellation of removal. Moreover, if a person receives special rule cancellation, then his or her spouse, child, and (if here by October 1, 1990) adult son or daughter may receive special rule cancellation as well. NACARA § 203(a,b).

To qualify for the special rule, the person has to have entered before a specified date in 1990. (The date varies depending on the applicant's nationality.) One must affirmatively apply. As noted earlier, the substantive requirements are virtually the same as those formerly in place under the pre-IIRAIRA version of suspension of deportation. The most important relaxations are the seven-year physical presence requirement (rather than the new requirement of ten years), the requirement of merely "extreme" hardship to oneself or one's family members (rather than the more demanding "exceptional and extremely unusual" hardship only to one's family members); and the inapplicability of the IIRAIRA rule that continuous physical presence ends with the filing of a notice to appear or with the commission of a designated crime. Note, however, that under even those more liberal rules, the remedy is still discretionary. There is no judicial review of a decision by the immigration judge or the BIA denying special rule cancellation. NACARA § 203(a)(1).

One significant recent development is the publication of the Justice Department's interim rules on NACARA. These took effect on June 21, 1999. 64 Fed. Reg. 27856 (May 21, 1999). The new rules create a rebuttable presumption of extreme hardship for most of the Guatemalans and Salvadorans (not the Soviets and Eastern Europeans) covered by NACARA. The presumption means that in applicable cases the INS has the burden of proving that removal will *not* cause extreme hardship to the applicant or to his or her citizen or permanent resident family members. The regulations suggest two ways to rebut the presumption -- by showing that there is no evidence at all of extreme hardship (e.g. no family members, work history, or other ties to the community); or by showing that the applicant has great wealth in his or her home country. *Id.* at 27865, amending 8 C.F.R. § 240.64(d). Approximately 240,000 Guatemalans and Salvadorans are expected to benefit from this presumption. 64 Fed. Reg. at 27865.

Even though the adjustments of status that result from NACARA are exempt from the 4000 limit, some of those grants -- namely, those to the Guatemalan and Salvadoran beneficiaries -- will eventually be deducted from the quotas available in future years for two other programs that you studied earlier. Under the statutory formula, one-half of the Guatemalan and Salvadoran adjustments are subtracted from the annual ceilings for diversity immigrants, and the other one-half from the annual ceilings for the "other workers" prong of the employment-based third preference category. In no event, however, may the reduction to either quota exceed 5000 in any given fiscal year. NACARA § 203(d). If the predictions that there will be several hundred thousand Guatemalan and Salvadoran applicants prove accurate, therefore, the maximum reductions of 5000 per year to the diversity and "other workers" programs will continue for many years.

For more detail on the substantive criteria and procedures under NACARA, see the statute, the regulations, and Mario M. Lovo, *Nicaraguan Adjustment and Central American Relief Act "NACARA"*, Nov. 1998 Immigration Briefings.

Page 502, after paragraph (c), add the following:

d. NICARAGUANS AND CUBANS IN 1997

In addition to creating the "special rule" cancellation discussed earlier, the Nicaraguan Adjustment and Central American Relief Act, Pub. L. 105-100, Title II, section 202, 111 Stat. 2160, 2193 (Nov. 19, 1997), or NACARA, established an amnesty program for certain Nicaraguan and Cuban nationals continuously physically present in the United States since December 1, 1995. (Absences of 180 days or less will not destroy the continuity.) The person must also be otherwise admissible, except that certain common inadmissibility grounds are made inapplicable. These include public charge, lack of labor certification, presence without admission, and inadequate documents. NACARA § 202(a,b). By virtue of a curative amendment, the inadmissibility grounds for aliens who have been out of status 180 days or one year, INA § 212(a)(9)(B), are also inapplicable. Technical Corrections to the Nicaraguan Adjustment and Central American Relief Act, Pub. L. 105-139, §§ 1(a)(2)(B), 1(b)(2)(C), 111 Stat. 2644 (Dec. 2, 1997), amending NACARA §§ 202(a)(1)(B),

202(d)(1)(D). Unlike the discretionary special rule cancellation section of NACARA, this program is mandatory; the Attorney General "shall" adjust the status of those applicants who meet all the requirements. NACARA § 202(a)(1). Applications must be filed before April 1, 2000. NACARA § 202(a)(1)(A). Approximately 150,000 Nicaraguans and 5,000 Cubans are expected to benefit. See Nadine Wettstein, *The Peddler Sells His Caps: The EOIR and INS Issue a New Rule on the Suspension/Cancellation Ceiling*, 3 Bender's Immigration Bulletin 1083 (Nov. 1, 1998).

Except when removal proceedings have already been instituted, applications under NACARA § 202 are filed with the INS Service Center in Texas. Administrative review by an immigration judge, and then by the BIA, is available as of right. The procedures are described in Mario Lovo, *Nicaraguan Adjustment and Central American Relief Act "NACARA"*, Nov. 1998 Immigration Briefings at 9. The statute expressly bars judicial review. NACARA § 202(f).

e. HAITIANS IN 1998

In granting amnesty to Nicaraguans and Cubans, and special rule cancellations of removal and adjustments of status to Guatemalans, Salvadorans, Soviets, and Eastern Europeans (see the earlier discussion), NACARA left a gaping hole. As you have seen, Haitian refugees have fled to the United States in significant numbers in recent years, and their plight seems every bit as desperate as that of the people covered by NACARA. After volatile public debate, Congress therefore enacted the Haitian Refugee Immigration Fairness Act of 1998, Pub. L. 105-277, Div. A, § 101(h), Title IX, 112 Stat. 2681 (Nov. 2, 1998). This legislation provides a legalization program, culminating in adjustment of status, for certain Haitian nationals who have resided in the United States since December 31, 1995 and who had applied for asylum or had been paroled before that date. Applications must be filed by April 1, 2000.

Pages 503-04, delete everything from the 1st full paragraph on page 503 through line 2 on page 504, and substitute the following:

As discussed in more detail in chapter 5, temporary legislation enacted in 1994 (the addition of INA § 245(i)) generally enabled otherwise eligible overstayers to qualify for adjustment by paying a penalty fee. The same was possibly true even for aliens who were present without admission. The lapsing of section 245(i) in January 1998 eliminated both possibilities. Consequently, the practical relevance of section 245 in removal proceedings today is mainly for aliens who were admitted as nonimmigrants, are deportable for overstaying or otherwise violating the terms of their admission, and are exempt from the out-of-status bar either because they are immediate relatives, INA § 245(c)(2), or because they are employment-based preference immigrants who have not been out of status more than 180 days, INA § 245(k).

Page 504, delete subsection 5 and substitute the following:

5. PRIVATE BILLS

One remedy of last resort is the "private bill" -- legislation that provides permanent resident status for a specific individual when existing general provisions would not. Excellent summaries of the history of, and criteria and procedures for, private bills include Robert Hopper & Juan P. Osuna, *Remedies of Last Resort: Private Bills and Deferred Action*, June 1997 Immigration Briefings; David Weissbrodt, Immigration Law and Procedure in a Nutshell 94-101 (4th ed. 1998).

Private immigration bills were once quite common. For one stretch during the 1960's, they constituted about 50% of all bills introduced in Congress -- several thousand each year. Hopper & Osuna, above, at 3. As a result of numerous scandals -- including the ABSCAM affair, in which an FBI sting operation caught several members of Congress accepting bribes from foreign business persons in exchange for the introduction of private bills -- both the number of such bills introduced and the number enacted have slowed to a trickle. In the two years of the 104th Congress (1995-96), only 14 private immigration bills were introduced and only two were enacted. *Id*.

Several commentators have suggested that IIRAIRA, by severely curtailing other discretionary relief from removal, might prompt at least a modest resurgence of private immigration legislation. *Id*; see also Weissbrodt, above, at 96. One recent high-profile example is the bill introduced by Rep. Bill McCollum, a Florida Republican, on behalf of the son of a powerful Republican party official. After serving four years in prison for 13 felony convictions on theft and fraud counts, the son had been ordered deported to Canada, his country of nationality. As a result of IIRAIRA's elimination of all other avenues of discretionary relief, existing law left him without a remedy. Having actively supported IIRAIRA, McCollum drew criticism for seeking relief on behalf of the friend of a party official. McCollum denied any political motive for the bill. Syndicated columnist Anthony Lewis observed "Congressman McCollum may be moved by the human consequences of the 1996 law now that he sees them. It is easy to be for harsh measures in the abstract. It is not so easy when you see the result in shattered lives." See Anthony Lewis, *Abroad at Home: The Quality of Mercy*, New York Times, Feb. 27, 1999 at A15.

The first step in obtaining a private immigration bill is persuading a member of Congress to introduce it. Once such bills are introduced, they are ordinarily routed to the immigration subcommittees of the Judiciary Committees of the respective Houses. Both subcommittees now have formal rules that lay out the procedures for, and discuss generally the substantive criteria for granting, private immigration legislation. The latest versions of those rules are reproduced in Hopper & Osuna, above, at 18-22.

Philosophically, what do you think of the concept of private immigration bills? What functions do they serve? What dangers do they present?

Page 508, after item 4, add new item 5:

5. For a good description of deferred action and some helpful practice pointers, see Robert Hopper & Juan P. Osuna, *Remedies of Last Resort: Private Bills and Deferred Action*, June 1997 Immigration Briefings at 9-12.

Page 508, before last paragraph, add the following:

The Justice Department regulations empower both the INS and the EOIR (immigration judges and the BIA) to grant voluntary departure, but in differing circumstances. The INS has authority to grant voluntary departure only under subsection (a) of section 240B -- i.e., only in lieu of removal proceedings or before their completion. 8 C.F.R. § 240.25. If proceedings have not yet commenced (because no Notice to Appear has yet been filed), then the INS simply grants voluntary departure on its own. If proceedings have commenced (with the filing of the Notice to Appear), and the INS agrees to voluntary departure, then it has two options. One option is to join with the alien in a motion to the immigration judge to dismiss the case. If the motion is granted, the INS may then grant voluntary departure. The other option is to join with the alien in requesting the immigration judge to grant voluntary departure, which he or she may then do. 8 C.F.R. § 240.25(d).

At a certain point, however, the immigration judge loses the power to grant voluntary departure under subsection (a) of section 240B. To explain what that point is, a brief detour is necessary.

Before holding a full removal hearing for an alien alleged to be deportable, an immigration judge normally schedules a shorter and less formal event called a "master calendar" hearing. The main purposes of the master calendar hearing are to complete certain preliminary tasks, get a sense of the complexity of the issues likely to arise, and to set a date and time for the full hearing. For more detail on master calendar hearings, see page 539 below.

Under the Justice Department regulations, an alien who applies to an immigration judge for voluntary departure under subsection (a) must apply either before or during the master calendar hearing. Moreover, the immigration judge may grant subsection (a) voluntary departure only up to 30 days after the master calendar hearing, unless the INS stipulates to such a grant some time before the completion of removal proceedings. 8 C.F.R. § 240.26(b). Thus, absent an INS stipulation, the only brand of voluntary departure that an immigration judge has the power to grant more than 30 days after the master calendar hearing (and note that the actual removal hearing is almost always more than 30 days later) is subsection (b) voluntary departure. 8 C.F.R. § 240.26(c). For that, the substantive requirements are more stringent and the maximum duration is shorter (60 days rather than 120 days). Under the statute, subsection (b) voluntary departure may be granted only "at the conclusion of" the removal hearing.

The voluntary departure provision is inartfully drafted. Subsection (a) purports to operate "prior to the completion" of removal proceedings. Taken alone, that provision implies, and the regulations discussed above similarly assume, that subsection (a) voluntary departure may be granted either before proceedings begin or while they are going on. In contrast, the more difficult subsection (b) voluntary departure may be granted only "at the conclusion" of removal proceedings. The problem is that a grant of voluntary departure ends the removal proceeding; by definition, it is *always* at the conclusion of the proceeding (assuming a proceeding has commenced). Under the literal wording, therefore, the portion of subsection (a) that authorizes voluntary departure "prior to completion" is useless. If proceedings have commenced but not finished, voluntary departure ends the proceedings and therefore would seem to be governed by subsection (b). The Justice Department regulations commendably take a nonliteral approach and allow the more lenient subsection (a) voluntary departure even after commencement of removal proceedings.

The timing distinctions drawn by the voluntary departure provisions are significant for another reason as well. Recall the "unlawful presence" exclusion that you studied in chapter 4. Under INA § 212(a)(9)(B)(i), an alien who was unlawfully present in the United States for more than 180 days but less than one year, and who "voluntarily departed . . . *prior to the commencement* of [removal] proceedings [emphasis added]" is inadmissible to return for three years. Whether one departs before or after the filing of the Notice to Appear therefore has legal significance, as the Problems below illustrate.

Page 510, Question 2, add at end:

Consider also an analogy offered by Nora Demleitner in a February 8, 1998 e-mail to the author. She compares the voluntary departure scheme to the federal criminal sentencing guidelines, which allow sentence reductions for defendants who plead guilty. The stated rationale is that such a person should be rewarded for "accepting responsibility" and for saving the time and expense of a trial.

Page 510, Problem 1, line 5:

After the word "removal", insert the word "proceedings."

Page 529, item 4, line 1:

Change "243(a)" to "241(b)(2)."

Page 533, after last paragraph, add new paragraph:

Professor Dan Kanstroom makes a strong argument for *more* fixed rules and *less* delegated discretion in immigration cases. See Daniel Kanstroom, *Surrounding the Hole in the Doughnut: Discretion and Deference in U.S. Immigration Law*, 71 Tulane L. Rev. 703 (1997) (also arguing for other ways to structure discretion, including judicial review).

CHAPTER 8

DEPORTATION PROCEDURE

Page 535, 2nd paragraph, next-to-last line:

Change "employers" to "employees."

Page 537, replace paragraph 1 with the following:

Once the INS decides to initiate removal proceedings against someone whom it has arrested, it has to decide whether to detain the person pending a final removal decision. The detention decision is extremely important, because removal proceedings typically take at least several months, and sometimes several years, to complete. Detention entails not only a loss of liberty for the detainee, but also impaired access to counsel, potential economic and other hardships for the detainee's family members, and of course great expense for the government. Stephen H. Legomsky, *The Detention of Aliens: Theories, Rules, and Discretion*, § 1, 30 U. Miami Inter-Amer. L. Rev., issue # 3 (forthcoming 1999).

Today, detention is *mandatory* for certain categories of aliens. In 1988, Congress required detention for aggravated felons (a category then defined narrowly) while deportation proceedings were pending. Pub. L. 100-690, §§ 7341, 7343(a), 7344, 102 Stat. 4181, 4469-71 (Nov. 18, 1988). The constitutionality of this legislation was considered earlier. See pages 87-89 of the casebook. In 1996, AEDPA and IIRAIRA combined to extend mandatory detention to several other major categories: (1) almost all aliens who are inadmissible or deportable on crime-related grounds (not just aggravated felons); (2) those who are inadmissible or deportable on terrorism grounds; (3) most arriving passengers (including those subject to expedited removal); and (4) aliens awaiting the execution of final removal orders. See INA §§ 235(b)(1)(B)(iii)(IV), 235(b)(2)(A), 236(c)(1)(A,B,C,D), 241(a)(1,2,3). These provisions have proved controversial. See generally Donald Kerwin, Eleanor Acer, and David Leopold, *The Detention of Noncitizens -- An Overview of the Law, Its Implementation, and Legal Strategies*, AILA, Immigration and Nationality Law Handbook (1999) (forthcoming); Donald Kerwin & Charles Wheeler, *The Detention Mandates of the 1996 Immigration Act: An Exercise in Overkill*, 75 Interpreter Releases 1433 (Oct. 19, 1998); Legomsky, above; Stanley Mailman & Stephen Yale-Loehr, *INS Detention Policies Criticized*, 3 Bender's Immigration Bulletin 1079 (Nov. 1, 1998); Peter H. Schuck, *INS Detention and Removal: A "White Paper"*, 11 Geo. Immigration L.J. 667 (1997); Margaret H. Taylor, *The 1996 Immigration Act: Detention and Related Issues*, 74 Interpreter Releases 209 (Feb. 3, 1997); Margaret H. Taylor, *Symbolic Detention*, 20 In Defense of the Alien 153 (1998); Vera Institute of Justice, The

Appearance Assistance Program (1998).

In all other cases the INS has the discretion whether to detain the person without bond, release the person on cash bond of at least $1500, or release the person on "conditional parole." INA § 236(a). Release is permitted only if the INS is satisfied that the individual "would not pose a danger to property or persons and * * * is likely to appear for any future proceeding." 8 C.F.R. § 236.1(c)(8) (1999).

On May 1, 1999 the INS took a controversial step, implementing a "Hub Site Detention and Removals Plan" for the 18-state Central Region. Under this plan, asylum seekers and other INS detainees are sent to "hub" detention facilities. Instead of detaining people in the facility nearest their home or their place of apprehension, the INS will now group the detainees by national origin. In the Central Region, Mexican, Central American, and Caribbean nationals will be moved to Texas; all others will be moved to Chicago. Immigrant advocates fear that the hubbing system will make it even harder for the detainees to obtain counsel, prevent visits from family members, and require increased use of county jails, where the detainees will be mixed in with criminal offenders. See 4 Bender's Immigration Bulletin 450 (May 15, 1999).

Page 539, after 1st full paragraph (i.e. the paragraph that ends "Is it justifiable?", add a new paragraph:

Under the Vienna Convention on Consular Relations, art. 5(i), 21 U.S.T. 77, 84, 596 U.N.T.S. 261, 268 (Apr. 24, 1963), consulates have the right to represent their own nationals before the tribunals of the host state. Because of a recent Memorandum of Understanding on Consular Protection of Mexican and United States Nationals (May 7, 1996) and an earlier settlement agreement in United States domestic litigation, U.S. immigration officials who believe an arrestee is unlawfully in the United States must notify the person of his or her right to communicate with the relevant consulate. For a good discussion, see Jorge A. Vargas, *Consular Protection to Illegal Migratory Workers and Mexican Undocumented Minors: Two Sensitive Issues Addressed by the Thirteenth Annual Meeting of the United States-Mexico Binational Commission*, 6 Fla. State Univ. J. Transnat'l L. & Policy 143 (1996).

Page 542, subsection 4, 1st paragraph, lines 6-8, replace the sentence that begins "It consists . . ." and corresponding citation with the following:

It now consists of up to eighteen permanent members, including a Chair and a Deputy Chair, all appointed by the Attorney General. 63 Fed. Reg. 51518 (Sept. 28, 1998).

Page 543, 1st paragraph, add at end:

The credibility issue has acquired special significance in the asylum context. For more detail, see the passages of this Supplement that correspond to casebook pages 871 and 875.

Page 543, after 3rd full paragraph, add the following:

In the same vein, the BIA has now issued a controversial proposed rule that would allow the Chairperson to authorize selected Board members to render one-member decisions "without opinion" in a wide variety of cases that the member believes do not raise significant factual or legal issues. In such cases, the order "shall not include further explanation or reasoning." 63 Fed. Reg. 49,043 (Sept. 14, 1998), proposing to add 8 C.F.R. § 3.1(a)(5). For a strenuous attack on the "without opinion" portion of the proposal, see Philip G. Schrag, *The Summary Affirmance Proposal of the Board of Immigration Appeals*, 12 Georgetown Immigration L.J. 531 (1998) (not necessarily objecting to the concept of one-member decisions).

At the other end of the spectrum, the Board in unusually important cases sometimes proceeds en banc. This used to mean that every Board member would participate in the decision. A recent regulation, however, permits the Board to render nine-member en banc decisions. 8 C.F.R. § 3.1(a)(4)(ii) (1999), added by 63 Fed. Reg. 31889 (June 15, 1998).

Page 552, change subsections ii, iii, and iv of the text of 8 C.F.R. § 292.1(a)(2), to reflect a Final Rule, 62 Fed. Reg. 23634 (May 1, 1997), as follows:

(ii) In the case of a law student, he or she has filed a statement that he or she is participating, under the direct supervision of a faculty member, licensed attorney, or accredited representative, in a legal aid program or clinic conducted by a law school or non-profit organization, and that he or she is appearing without direct or indirect remuneration from the alien he or she represents;

(iii) In the case of a law graduate, he or she has filed a statement that he or she is appearing under the supervision of a licensed attorney or accredited representative and that he or she is appearing without direct or indirect remuneration from the alien he or she represents; and

(iv) The law student's or law graduate's appearance is permitted by the official before whom he or she wishes to appear (namely an immigration judge, district director, officer-in-charge, regional director, the Commissioner, or the Board). The official or officials may require that a law student be accompanied by the supervising faculty member, attorney, or accredited representative.

Page 556, item 4, 1st paragraph, add at end:

In 1997 these interim regulations became final. 62 Fed. Reg. 23634 (May 1, 1997). The changes are reflected in the version of 8 C.F.R. § 292.1(a)(2) that appears in the passage of this Supplement corresponding to casebook page 552.

Page 556, item 5, add at end:

For an update, see Donald Kerwin, *Charitable Legal Immigration Programs: Can They Survive?*, 74 Interpreter Releases 813 (May 19, 1997).

Page 557, add new item 6A:

6A. In early 1998 the Justice Department published several proposed changes to the disciplinary rules that you have just read. 63 Fed. Reg. 2901 (Jan. 20, 1998). Some of those changes either reword or reorganize the existing grounds, generally by tracking the language found in analogous provisions of the ABA Model Rules of Professional Conduct (1995). Other proposed changes would add new grounds, applicable only to practice before the BIA and the immigration judges (not the INS). These include "repeatedly fail[ing] to appear at scheduled hearings in a timely manner", 63 Fed. Reg. at 2906, proposing to add 8 C.F.R. § 3.52(l), and ineffective assistance of counsel (discussed in item 8 of the Notes and Questions below.) Still other proposed changes, which would affect the procedures, are discussed in item 9 of these Notes and Questions. At this writing, the proposed rules have not yet been adopted.

Page 557, item 8, add the following:

The proposed rules address this issue. They would discipline any practitioner who "[e]ngages in conduct that constitutes ineffective assistance of counsel, as previously determined in a finding by the Board or the Immigration Court in an immigration proceeding, within five years preceding the filing of the complaint." 63 Fed. Reg. at 2906, proposing to add 8 C.F.R. § 3.52(k). The Department's expressed concern is that under present law an alien can move to reopen removal proceedings on the basis of ineffective assistance of counsel, and the counsel in question can then admit having been ineffective without incurring any consequences. 63 Fed. Reg. at 2902. The objective of the new rule appears to be to discourage the filing of motions to reopen based on alleged ineffective assistance, rather than to deter or sanction the ineffectiveness. Do you see any dangers in disciplining immigration practitioners for ineffective assistance?

Page 557, after item 8, add new item 8A:

8A. As you saw in chapter 6, ineffective assistance of counsel will not usually be a basis for withdrawing a guilty plea in criminal proceedings unless the ineffectiveness prejudiced the defendant. In a disciplinary proceeding against a practitioner for alleged ineffective assistance of counsel, should the government be required to prove prejudice?

Page 557, item 9, add a 3rd paragraph:

The Justice Department's proposed rules also revamp the procedures for investigating and adjudicating disciplinary cases against private attorneys and representatives. (Complaints against government attorneys would still be decided by the Office of Professional Responsibility.) Under the proposed new procedures, a complaint against the alien's attorney or representative would be filed with the Office of the General Counsel of either the INS or the EOIR, depending on the setting in which the alleged misconduct occurred. The relevant Office of General Counsel would then decide whether to initiate proceedings. If it does, the Director of EOIR would appoint an "adjudicating official," who would then hold a hearing. If the adjudicating official finds the alleged grounds established by "clear, unequivocal, and convincing evidence," he or she would recommend a disciplinary sanction to a three-member "Disciplinary Committee" appointed by the Deputy Attorney General. That committee would make a de novo decision. See generally 63 Fed. Reg. at 2904-11.

During the notice and comment period, the ABA objected to the entire structure of the proposed rules. As you will recall, it is the ABA whose Model Code and Model Rules are in place in the 50 states. The ABA position is that, since lawyers are already subject to state ethical rules, additional Justice Department rules are unnecessary, except for nonlawyer representatives. Instead, the ABA argues, complaints about lawyer conduct in immigration cases should simply be referred to the appropriate state authorities. In any event, the ABA feels, the procedures for government lawyers should be the same as those for private lawyers. In particular, the ABA objects that the same federal agency that is lodging the complaint would be investigating the lawyer who is opposing it -- a recipe for unfair prosecution. See letter from ABA President Robert D. Evans to Ms. Margaret M. Philbin, EOIR General Counsel (Mar. 23, 1998).

Page 565, last full paragraph, Taylor article, change citation to read:

Margaret H. Taylor, *Promoting Legal Representation for Detained Aliens: Litigation and Administrative Reform*, 29 Connecticut L. Rev. 1647 (1997).

Page 595, item 5, add a 2nd paragraph:

In *Hodgers-Durgin v. de la Vina*, 165 F.3d 667 (9th Cir. 1999), persons who alleged that their vehicles had been stopped by the Border Patrol solely because of the occupants' Hispanic appearance brought a class action against Border Patrol officials for injunctive and declaratory relief. A Ninth Circuit panel held that the named plaintiffs had standing to bring the action and that a class action was appropriate. The Ninth Circuit has now vacated that decision, however, in order to rehear the case en banc. *Hodgers-Durgin v. de la Vina*, No. 97-16449 (May 13, 1999).

Page 595, add new item 6:

6. In *United States v. Verdugo-Urquidez*, 494 U.S. 259 (1990), the Supreme Court held that the Fourth Amendment does not apply to searches and seizures of the property of nonresident aliens outside the United States. Professor Victor Romero sees a common thread in this case and *Lopez-Mendoza*. See Victor C. Romero, *Whatever Happened to the Fourth Amendment? Undocumented Immigrants' Rights after INS v. Lopez-Mendoza and United States v. Verdugo-Urquidez*, 65 So. Cal. L. Rev. 999 (1992). In *United States v. Alvarez-Machain*, 504 U.S. 655 (1992), the Court went a step further. It held that the U.S. government's forcible abduction of a Mexican national from Mexico did not violate the United States-Mexico extradition treaty and did not destroy the criminal jurisdiction of the United States court.

Page 596, after 2nd full paragraph, add:

The Supreme Court has now ruled, however, that the Fifth Amendment privilege against self-incrimination does not protect against the threat of *foreign* prosecution. See *United States v. Balsys*, 524 U.S. 666 (1998); Irene Scharf, *Commentary on United States v. Balsys*, 3 Bender's Immigration Bulletin 886 (Sept. 1, 1998).

Page 621, before last paragraph, add the following heading:

i. Crime-Related Removal Orders

Pages 621-22, delete the bracketed sentence and corresponding citation to Ter Yang, and substitute the following:

On that issue, the courts are divided. In *Ter Yang v. INS*, 109 F.3d 1185 (7th Cir. 1997), the court held that it had jurisdiction to determine whether it had jurisdiction. Since jurisdiction hinged on whether the alien was deportable, the court reasoned, it had the power to decide whether that jurisdictional fact was present. Accord, *Xiong v. INS*, 173 F.3d 601 (7th Cir. 1999). But in *Berehe v. INS*, 114 F.3d 159 (10th Cir. 1997), another court rejected the 7th Circuit view, holding that for jurisdictional purposes deportability can be determined by the administrative authorities. Whether Congress can constitutionally preclude judicial review of the administrative decision is another question, taken up below.

On a separate issue, the Ninth Circuit has held that, when it lacks jurisdiction to review a removal order based on a criminal conviction, it also lacks jurisdiction to review the denial of a motion to reopen or reconsider. *Beltran-Leon v. INS*, 134 F.3d 1379 (9th Cir. 1998).

ii. Denials of Discretionary Relief

Page 622, last paragraph, line 3:

Change "241(c)" to "241(b)(3)".

Page 623, after 3rd full paragraph, add a new paragraph:

Recent cases have adopted the approach that the preceding considerations suggest. IIRAIRA § 309(c) established certain transition rules for aliens whose exclusion or deportation proceedings were pending on the date of enactment. Under section 309(c)(4)(E), if such an alien is ordered excluded or deported more than 30 days after enactment, "there shall be no appeal of any discretionary decision under [specified INA sections]." This language resembles the phrase "decision or action * * * in the discretion of the Attorney General" found in permanent INA § 242(a)(2)(B)(ii). At least two circuits have interpreted the transition language to bar only the discretionary portions of the determinations, and not findings of fact or conclusions of law concerning the person's statutory eligibility for relief. See *Moosa v. INS*, 171 F.3d 994, 1010-13 (5th Cir. 1999); *Antonio-Cruz v. INS*, 147 F.3d 1129, 1130 (9th Cir. 1998). For a thoughtful criticism of the statutory bar on judicial review of discretionary determinations, see Daniel Kanstroom, *Surrounding the Hole in the Doughnut: Discretion and Deference in U.S. Immigration Law*, 71 Tulane L. Rev. 703 (1997).

iii. Expedited Removal Orders

Page 624, after 1st full paragraph, add the following heading:

iv. Voluntary Departure Regulations

Page 624, after 2d full paragraph, add the following:

v. Prosecutorial Discretion

Yet another court-stripping provision requires more detailed discussion. INA § 242(g) provides:

> Except as provided in this section and notwithstanding any other provision of law, no court shall have jurisdiction to hear any cause or claim by or on behalf of any alien arising from the decision or action by the Attorney General to commence proceedings, adjudicate cases, or execute removal orders against any alien under this Act.

In *Reno v. American-Arab Anti-Discrimination Committee*, 119 S.Ct. 936 (1999), the Supreme Court wrestled with the meaning of this provision. Both parties had assumed that the claims barred by section 242(g) included the review of practically every order arising from a removal proceeding, including the removal order itself. But that assumption generated a dilemma. Under IIRAIRA § 309(c)(1), the old -- i.e., pre-section 242 -- judicial review provisions govern cases pending at the time of the enactment. By way of exception, however, IIRAIRA § 306(c)(1) provides that new section 242(g) applies even to pending cases. And section 242(g) says that "except as provided *in this section*" (emphasis added), presumably meaning section 242, the specified actions are unreviewable. Thus, if the parties' assumption is correct -- i.e., if section 242(g) bars review of removal orders except pursuant to the procedures prescribed by the rest of section 242 -- then there is no authority at all for reviewing removal orders in cases that were pending at the time of enactment. That is because IIRAIRA § 309(c)(1) expressly made the rest of section 242 inapplicable to pending cases. That result seems implausible, since Congress in restricting judicial review obviously had no reason to treat pending cases *less* favorably than future cases. Conversely, to interpret the "except" clause in section 242 as permitting judicial review under the old provisions would render IIRAIRA § 309(c)(1) meaningless.

The Court's solution was to give section 242(g) its literal meaning. The statutory reference to claims "arising from the decision or action of the Attorney General to commence proceedings, adjudicate cases, or execute removal orders" was narrowly construed to bar review only of those three specific decisions. One central purpose of the legislation, the Court said, was to bar review of the INS's prosecutorial discretion, as in cases denying deferred action. Under that interpretation, for example, the removal order itself does not arise from those decisions or actions and thus is not affected by section 242(g). See 119 S.Ct. at 940-45.

This narrow construction did not help the plaintiffs in *Reno*, who sought to enjoin removal proceedings on the ground of selective prosecution. Even under a narrow interpretation, the Court held that section 242(g) bars judicial review of the Attorney General's decisions to commence proceedings -- precisely the decisions the plaintiffs were challenging. As you will see below, however, the Court's interpretation of section 242(g) could be highly significant in another context -- the use of habeas corpus to challenge otherwise unreviewable removal orders in criminal cases.

vi. Detention Decisions

One last court-stripping provision relates to detention. While removal proceedings are pending, the Attorney General has the discretion whether to detain the alien, release him or her on bond, or grant parole without requiring bond. INA § 236(a). By way of exception, detention is mandatory for most aliens deportable on criminal grounds. INA § 236(c). Under INA § 236(e), "[n]o court may set aside any action or decision of the Attorney General under this section regarding the detention or release of any alien or the grant, revocation, or denial of bond or parole."

While section 236(e) literally bars review of the Attorney General's decisions implementing section 236, some courts have held that this provision does not bar the use of habeas corpus to challenge the constitutionality of section 236 itself. See *Parra v. Perryman*, 172 F.3d 954 (7th Cir. 1999); *Van Eeton v. Beebe*, CV 99-16-PA (D. Oreg., Apr. 13, 1999). Those two courts ultimately divided on the merits; the court in *Parra* upheld the constitutionality of mandatory detention, while the court in *Van Eeton* held it violative of both substantive and procedural due process. Section 236(e) aside, an earlier 11th Circuit decision had held that INA § 242(g), discussed above, barred the use of habeas to challenge detention. *Richardson v. Reno*, 162 F.3d 1338 (11th Cir. 1998). But the Supreme Court, in the light of its decision in *Reno v. American-Arab Anti-Discrimination Committee* narrowly construing section 242(g), vacated the decision in *Richardson*. See *Richardson v. Reno*, No. 98-1361 (June 1, 1999).

Pages 624-25, delete the heading for subsection (c) and the two introductory paragraphs, and substitute the following:

c. OTHER SOURCES OF JURISDICTION

When a petition for review under INA § 242 is precluded, are there other sources of subject matter jurisdiction for reviewing either final removal orders or other miscellaneous decisions related to the removal process? Section 242(a)(1) says: "Judicial review of a final order of removal [other than expedited removal] is governed *only* by [the petition for review procedure]" (emphasis added).

Should this exclusivity language be read literally, to bar even habeas corpus and general federal question jurisdiction? And if so, is a total bar on judicial review constitutional? The materials that follow address those questions.

Page 631, 1st full paragraph, replace postscript with the following:

Postscript: The INS has now conceded, and several courts of appeals have agreed, that section 242 does not bar the use of habeas corpus under 28 U.S.C. § 2241 to challenge the legality of removal orders, at least when those challenges pose substantial constitutional questions. See, e.g., *Goncalves v. Reno*, 144 F.3d 110 (1st Cir. 1998); *Henderson v. INS*, 157 F.3d 106 (2d Cir. 1998); *Sandoval v. Reno*, 166 F.3d 225 (3rd Cir. 1999); *Nguyen v. INS*, 117 F.3d 206 (5th Cir. 1997); *Mansour v. INS*, 123 F.3d 423 (6th Cir. 1997); *Mayers v. INS*, No. 97-5537 (11th Cir., May 20, 1999); *Ramallo v. Reno*, 114 F.3d 1210 (D.C. Cir. 1997). In contrast, the Seventh Circuit interprets section 242 as prohibiting habeas corpus review of removal orders. To avoid constitutional questions about Congress's power to bar all judicial review, however, the Seventh Circuit allows petitions for review, even for crime-related removal orders, when the petitions raise substantial constitutional issues. See *Singh v. Reno*, No. 98-3584 (7th Cir., May 26, 1999); *LaGuerre v. INS*, 164 F.3d 1035 (7th Cir. 1998). Still uncertain is the availability of habeas corpus to review most crime-related removal orders when the challenges are predicated on nonconstitutional grounds, such as statutory interpretation questions or issues of the sufficiency of the evidence.

There has been some fine recent commentary on this subject. See, e.g., Lenni Benson, *The New World of Judicial Review of Removal Orders*, 12 Georgetown Immigration L.J. 233 (1998); Lenni Benson, *Back to the Future: Congress Attacks the Right to Judicial Review of Immigration Proceedings*, 29 Conn. L. Rev. 1411 (1997); David Cole, *Jurisdiction and Liberty: Habeas Corpus and Due Process as Limits on Congress's Control of Federal Jurisdiction*, 86 Georgetown L.J. 2481 (1998); Richard H. Fallon, *Applying the Suspension Clause to Immigration Cases*, 98 Colum. L. Rev. 1068 (1998); M. Isabel Medina, *Judicial Review -- A Nice Thing? Article III, Separation of Powers and the Illegal Immigration Reform and Immigrant Responsibility Act of 1996*, 29 Conn. L. Rev. 1525 (1997); Gerald L. Neuman, *Habeas Corpus, Executive Detention, and the Removal of Aliens*, 98 Colum. L. Rev. 961 (1998); Kathleen M. Sullivan, *Commentary on Reno v. American-Arab Anti-Discrimination Committee*, 4 Bender's Immigration Bulletin 249 (Mar. 15, 1999).

Page 631, before subsection (iii) on injunctions and class actions, insert the

following new heading:

d. OTHER REMEDIES

Pages 631-45, renumber headings as follows:

(1) On page 631, subsection (iii) becomes subsection (i).

(2) On page 633, subsections (iv), (v), and (d) become subsections (ii), (iii), and (e), respectively.

(3) On page 645, subsection (e) becomes subsection (f).

Page 711, after item 11, add new item 12:

The Justice Department has recently taken several steps to tame the BIA's burgeoning caseload. These include increasing the Board's authorized size from 15 members to 18, allowing limited en banc decisions, and issuing a proposed rule that would permit single-member decisions without written opinions. See the passages of this Supplement corresponding to pages 542 and 543 of the casebook.

Page 732, 1st full paragraph, line 5, before "sentencing," add the word "federal." [Thanks to Professor Estelle Lau for this observation.]

Pages 732-33, delete the last paragraph on p. 732 (starting with "A second source . . .") to the middle of p. 733 (ending with the Ogboman citation), and substitute the following:

From 1994 until the enactment of IIRAIRA in 1996, federal district judges could also order deportation as a condition for "supervised release" -- a kind of probation that may follow completion of confinement. 18 U.S.C. § 3583(d). But IIRAIRA created INA § 240(a)(3), which made administrative removal proceedings the exclusive means for deciding whether to remove aliens from the United States. Consequently, the courts no longer have the power to order removal as a condition of supervised release. Note, however, that section 240(a)(3) expressly preserves judicial removal under the INA § 238 procedure just discussed.

CHAPTER 9

REFUGEES

Page 748, footnote 1, add at end:

See also the web site of the United Nations High Commissioner for Refugees, http://www.unhcr.ch.

Page 749, 1st paragraph, add at end:

See also U.S. Commission on Immigration Reform, U.S. Refugee Policy: Taking Leadership 38 (June 6, 1997) (humanitarianism and promotion of human rights should guide refugee policy).

Page 749, 1st full paragraph, add at end:

Ideology aside, to what extent do ethnic considerations drive refugee policy? See Maryellen Fullerton, *Hungary, Refugees, and the Law of Return*, 8 Int'l J. Refugee L. 499 (1996) (criticizing Hungary for using refugee program mainly as "law of return").

Page 758, 1st paragraph, delete last sentence and corresponding citation, and substitute the following:

As of December 31, 1998, some 128 nations had signed both the 1951 Convention and the 1967 Protocol. Another 8 had signed one but not the other. 17 Refugee Survey Quarterly No. 4 at 232-36 (1998).

Page 762, chart at top, add two more rows:

Fiscal Year	**Authorizations**
1998	83,000
1999	78,000

Page 762, footnote 3, column 1, line 10, at the sentence break, add the following:

For 1998, see 62 Fed. Reg. 53219-20 (Oct. 10, 1997). For 1999, see 63 Fed. Reg. 55001-02 (Oct. 13, 1998).

Page 764, 1st full paragraph, add at end:

For a thoughtful comment on how refugee-receiving states have reacted to the end of the Cold War, see Julie Mertus, *The State and the Post-Cold War Refugee Regime: New Models, New Questions*, 20 Mich. J. Int'l L. 59 (1998).

Page 765, 1st paragraph:

(1) In line 3, change the list of countries to read "Africa, Bosnia, Burma, Cuba, Iran, Former Soviet Union, and Vietnam."

(2) Change "December 31, 1995" to "December 1998."

Page 766, after item 2, add new item 2A:

2A. Several leading commentators, finding the existing world refugee system inadequate on multiple fronts, have recently advocated multinational forms of temporary protection, commonly known as "burden-sharing". Peter Schuck, for example, argues for regional arrangements whereby states agree on burden-sharing criteria, delegate to an international agency the task of assigning quotas to the various signatories based on those criteria, try to recruit additional signatories, and freely trade quotas for money or other concessions. See Peter H. Schuck, *Refugee Burden-Sharing: A Modest Proposal*, 22 Yale J. Int'l L. 243 (1997). James Hathaway and R. Alexander Neve argue that the leading causes of nations' increasing reluctance to admit refugees have been the perception that refugee programs can become back doors for voluntary migrants and a belief that the burdens have been unequal. Their blueprint calls not only for regional agreements, but also for other "interest-convergence group" initiatives. James C. Hathaway & R. Alexander Neve, *Making International Refugee Law Relevant Again: A Proposal for Collectivized and Solution-Oriented Protection*, 10 Harv. Human Rights J. 115 (1997). Both approaches are summarized, and then criticized for accepting cultural discrimination by states, in Satvinder Juss, *Toward a Morally Legitimate Form of Refugee Law: The Uses of Cultural Jurisprudence*, 11 Harv. Human Rights J. 311 (1998).

Other prominent commentators agree that national procedures have impeded protection but reject both the premise that individualized adjudication is the culprit and the proffered solutions. See Deborah Anker, Joan Fitzpatrick & Andrew Shacknove, *Crisis and Cure: A Reply to Hathaway/Neve and Schuck*, 11 Harv. Human Rights J.

295 (1998). The Commission on Immigration Reform and many others have also urged the formation of regional "burden-sharing" schemes in which nations collectively provide temporary protection for those who need it but who do not meet the Convention definition of "refugee." See U.S. Commission on Immigration Reform, U.S. Refugee Policy: Taking Leadership 20-25 (June 1997); Forced Migration Project, Open Society Institute, A Proposal to Establish a Temporary Refuge Scheme in the Caribbean Region for Refugee and Migration Emergencies (1995); Susan Martin, Andy Schoenholtz & Deborah Waller Meyers, *Temporary Protection: Towards a New Regional and Domestic Framework*, 12 Georgetown Immigration L.J. 543, 559-66 (1998). The subject is important enough that the Executive Committee of UNHCR (EXCOM) made it the 1998 annual theme. For EXCOM's discussions and reports, see 17 Refugee Survey Quarterly No. 4 at 1-221 (1998).

Page 767, 1st paragraph, add at end:

Children face several forms of child-specific persecution and special problems in demonstrating even adult-style persecution. For a thoughtful discussion, see Jacqueline Bhabha & Wendy A. Young, *Through a Child's Eyes: Protecting the Most Vulnerable Asylum Seekers*, 75 Interpreter Releases 757 (June 1, 1998).

Page 767, item 8, add at end:

See U.S. Commission on Immigration Reform, U.S. Refugee Policy: Taking Leadership 35-37 (June 1997) (urging elimination of one-year waiting period and immediate grant of permanent resident status).

Page 768, after item 12, add new item 13:

Horrendous events in the Serbian province of Kosovo have prompted the most recent massive refugee flow. The Serbian police and armed forces attempted to crush the Kosovar rebellion and to effectuate an "ethnic cleansing" of the ethnic Albanian population. On March 24, 1999, NATO began an intensive bombing campaign. The Serbs' immediate response was to accelerate the atrocities. There followed a massive refugee flow, primarily into Albania and Macedonia. Overall, the refugees numbered in the hundreds of thousands. Several hundred thousand others were internally displaced within Kosovo. The nature of the atrocities and the scale of the exodus caught virtually all governments and international organizations by surprise. Albania responded generously, but Macedonia staunchly resisted.

The United States accepted 20,000 Kosovars who had fled temporily to Macedonia, mainly those with family members in the United States and those who were believed to be especially vulnerable. At first, the plan was to house the refugees on Guantanamo. The intention was to highlight the temporary nature of the refuge, so as not to reinforce Serbia's ethnic cleansing efforts. For various reasons the United States eventually changed course and resettled the Kosovars with American families. See generally U.S. Committee for Refugees, 20 Refugee Reports No. 4 (March/April 1999).

In the meantime, the bombing was taking its toll on Serbia. In June 1999, a peace accord was signed. The Serbs agreed to withdraw their troops, allow a NATO-dominated international peacekeeping force to occupy Kosovo, and permit the return of the Kosovars. At this writing, Serb troops have withdrawn and NATO and Russian troops are entering. Many refugees, still wary, plan not to return until the Serb troops have left, land mines are cleared, and it seems safe to come home. See Elisabeth Bumiller, *Frightened Kosovars Won't Rush Back Home*, New York Times (June 11, 1999).

Page 768, footnote 4:

(1) In column 1, line 4, change the year for the Anker cite from "1994" to "1999."

(2) At the end of the footnote, add the following:

For general commentary on the definition of "refugee", see Daniel J. Steinbock, *Interpreting the Refugee Definition*, 45 UCLA L. Rev. 733 (1998); Dirk Vanheule, *A Comparison of the Judicial Interpretations of the Notion of Refugee*, in Jean-Yves Carlier & Dirk Vanheule (eds.), Europe and Refugees: A Challenge?, chap. 5 (1997) (a comparison of the refugee definitions in 15 countries).

Page 779, after item 4, add new item 4A:

4A. The Fifth Circuit has said that an act is not "persecution" unless it is intended to inflict harm or punishment. *Faddoul v. INS*, 37 F.3d 185, 188 (5th Cir. 1994). The Ninth Circuit expressly rejected that view in *Pitcherskaia v. INS*, 118 F.3d 641 (1997). There, the Russian government purportedly attempted to "cure" homosexuality by forcible institutionalization, electroshock treatments, and drug-injections. The court held this to be persecution. The plaintiff was not required to prove that the Russian government wished to harm or punish her. The same holding can be inferred from *Matter of Kasinga*, I.D. 3278 (BIA, June 13, 1996) (female genital mutilation held to be persecution), discussed in the social group materials below.

Page 780,item 6, line 5, at sentence break, add the following:

Under proposed rules published in June 1998, relocation within the country of persecution would not be expected if there is a "reasonable possibility" of "other serious harm" (meaning serious harm other than persecution on one of the five statutory grounds). See 63 Fed. Reg. 31945, 31949 (June 11, 1998), proposing to add 8 C.F.R. § 208.13(b)(3).

Page 788, at end of item 6, add the following:

In *Matter of C-Y-Z-*, I.D. 3319 (BIA, June 4, 1997), the Board granted nonreturn under this provision to an alien whom the Chinese authorities had sterilized, even though there obviously was no fear of future sterilization. As you will see later, past persecution triggers a presumption of future persecution which, under than existing regulations, the INS could have rebutted only by showing changed country conditions. 8 C.F.R. § 208.16(b)(2)(1997). Proposed regulations would allow the INS to rebut the presumption through any evidence that showed the absence of the required well-founded fear. See 63 Fed. Reg. 31945, 31949 (June 11, 1998), proposing to add 8 C.F.R. § 208.16(b)(1)(A).

The Board in *C-Y-Z-* also granted asylum but conditioned it upon the INS determining that the 1000 limit had not yet been exceeded. The Board declined to decide whether the cap applied to the grant of asylum or only to the subsequent adjustment of status, inviting the Attorney General to settle that question by issuing definitive regulations. See also Katherine L. Vaughns, *Retooling the "Refugee" Definition: The New Immigration Reform Law's Impact on United States Domestic Asylum Policy*, 1 Rutgers Race & L. Rev. 41 (1998) (questioning wisdom of special legislation to benefit particular group for ideological reasons); Mary Crock, *Apart from Us or a Part of Us? Immigrants' Rights, Public Opinion and the Rule of Law*, 10 Int'l J. Refugee L. 49 (1998) (detailing responses of Australian courts to Chinese asylum claims based on fear of coerced sterilization and abortion).

Page 789, 1st full paragraph, line 11, at sentence break:

Cf. *Matter of O-Z and I-Z*, I.D. 3346 (BIA, Apr. 2, 1998) (persecution against Ukrainian Jews held to be on account of "nationality").

Page 789, at end of subsection (a), add the following:

The International Religious Freedom Act of 1998, Pub. L. 105-292, 112 Stat. 2787 (Oct. 27, 1998) [IRFA], has potential ramifications for aliens in fear of persecution on religious grounds. The Act creates, in the State Department, a new Office on International Religious Freedom, charged with monitoring religious persecution around the world. The Office will also assist the Secretary of State in preparing its annual Human Rights Reports and a separate "Annual Report on International Religious Freedom." IRFA §§ 101, 102. The latter is to be used by all who adjudicate asylum cases. *Id.* 601. IRFA also establishes a Commission on International Religious Freedom, which will will report annually for four years on the state of religious freedom overseas. *Id.* §§ 201-06. In addition, the statute requires training for all Justice Department and State Department personnel involved in refugee adjudication. See *id.* §§ 602(a)(adding INA § 207(f) for Justice Department adjudicators) and 602(b) (for foreign service officers).

Page 795, item 7, between the two paragraphs, add the following:

In *Matter of R-A-*, I.D. 3403 (BIA, June 11, 1999), the asylum applicant was a Guatemalan woman whose husband had subjected her to extreme, prolonged physical and mental abuse. The police would not protect her. She argued, among other things, that her husband was harming her in order to overcome her resistance to his male domination. The claim was one of imputed political opinion.

The Board found her testimony credible and found she had a well-founded fear of persecution. But the Board also concluded that there was no nexus between the persecution she feared and any political opinion her husband might impute to her. There was no evidence, the Board said, that he cared what her political opinions were.

Since the case arose in the Ninth Circuit, the Board had to distinguish *Lazo-Majano*. To do so, it read *Lazo-Majano* as standing only for the proposition that cynically imputed political opinion can suffice. Here, the Board believed, the persecution could not be linked to any imputed political opinion, cynical or otherwise.

In *Lazo-Majano*, however, the court had provided two other, independent rationales for the result. The court had treated the persecutor as seeking to overcome Lazo-Majano's actual political opinion that men should not be permitted to dominate women. In addition, the court had reasoned, Lazo-Majano's flight from persecution was itself an expression of political opinion, for which her tormentor would now persecute her if she were to return. But the Board declined to recognize those holdings, on the theory that they were inconsistent with *Elias-Zacarias*. There were, the Board said, no post-*Elias-Zacarias* cases in the Ninth Circuit confirming that those aspects of *Lazo-Majano* were still good law.

The Board's decision in *Matter of R-A-* also has large implications for the social group prong of the refugee definition. These issues are discussed in the Supplement passages corresponding to casebook page 811, item 11A, below.

Page 795, item 8, add at end:

For effective criticisms of *Elias-Zacarias*, and in particular the Court's failure to consider international interpretations of "persecution on account of political opinion," see Carolyn Patty Blum, *A Question of Values: Continuing Divergences Between U.S. and International Refugee Norms*, 15 Berkeley J. Int'l L. 1, 38, 41-42 (1997); Joan Fitzpatrick, *The International Dimension of U.S. Refugee Law*, 15 Berkeley J. Int'l L. 1, 20-24 (1997); Jennifer Moore, *Restoring the Humanitarian Character of U.S. Refugee Law Lessons from the International Community*, 15 Berkeley J. Int'l L. 51, 59-61 (1997).

Page 809, item 2, add at end:

Penelope Mathew, *The High Court and "Particular Social Groups": Lessons for the Future*, 21 Melbourne Univ. L. Rev. 277 (1997) (Australian High Court's approach to social groups).

Page 811, replace item 11 with the following two new items:

11. On the question of what "social group" means, most courts of appeals have favored the *Acosta* immutability test. The First Circuit, adopting that approach, has held that the nuclear family constitutes a particular social group. See *Gebremichael v. INS*, 10 F.3d 28, 36 (1st Cir. 1993). The Third Circuit has also adopted *Acosta*. See *Fatin v. INS*, 12 F.3d 1233 (3d Cir. 1993)(women constitute a social group, though no evidence in this case that applicant would be persecuted solely because of her gender). So has the Seventh Circuit. See *Lwin v. INS*, 144 F.3d 505, 511-12 (7th Cir. 1998) (parents of Burmese dissidents are social group). Both the Canadian Supreme Court and the British House of Lords have also rejected *Sanchez-Trujillo* in favor of *Acosta*. See *Matter of Attorney General and Ward*, 103 D.L.R.4th 1, 24-38 (Canadian S.Ct, 1993); *Islam (A.P.) v. Secretary of State for the Home Dept.*, [1999] 2 All E.R. 545, [1999] 2 W.L.R. 1015 (U.K. H.L. 1999) (all Pakistani women constitute a social group).

No other circuits have expressly adopted the Ninth Circuit test. The Second Circuit cited *Sanchez-Trujillo* with apparent approval but went on to follow a third approach. In *Gomez v. INS*, 947 F.2d 660, 664 (9th Cir. 1991), the court held that "social group" requires a common fundamental characteristic that is recognizable to its persecutors and to the outside world. Accord, *Saleh v. USDOJ*, 962 F.2d 234, 240 (2d Cir. 1992).

For some effective criticisms of the limitations announced in both *Acosta* and

Sanchez-Trujillo, see Maureen Graves, *From Definition to Exploration: Social Groups and Political Asylum Eligibility*, 26 San Diego L.Rev. 740 (1989).

11A. Given the rationale and the popularity of the *Acosta* test, the decision in *Matter of R-A-*, I.D. 3403 (BIA en banc, June 11, 1999), shocked immigration observers. A Guatemalan woman who had been the victim of persistent, extreme spousal violence applied for asylum. Both the immigration judge and the BIA believed her horrifying story and concluded she had a well-founded fear of future persecution. The issue before the Board was whether the persecution would be "on account of" one of the statutory bases. Earlier you encountered her claim of imputed political opinion. She also argued, however, that she would be persecuted because of her membership in a particular social group, which she defined as "Guatemalan women who have been involved intimately with Guatemalan male companions, who believe that women are to live under male domination."

Since the case arose in the Ninth Circuit, the Board was bound by *Sanchez-Trujillo*. Having concluded that the class she described lacked a "voluntary associational relationship," the Board held that this class of people did not constitute a social group. The vote was 10-5.

The Board could have stopped there. Had it done so, the holding would have been confined to the Ninth Circuit. *Acosta* would still govern elsewhere.

Instead, the Board added "Moreover, regardless of Ninth Circuit law, we find that the respondent's claimed social group fails under our own independent assessment of what constitutes a qualifying social group." The Board proceeded to describe *Acosta* as setting out only threshold conditions for meeting the social group definition. Once it is determined that membership in a group is immutable within the meaning of *Acosta*, the adjudicator should take other considerations into account.

In that vein, the Board said "[T]here must also be some showing of how the characteristic is understood in the alien's society, such that we in turn may understand that the potential persecutors in fact see persons sharing the characteristic as warranting suppression or the infliction of harm." (This point seems to bring the test closer to the Second Circuit formulation discussed in item 11 above.) In addition, the Board suggested, while its precedents do not require a voluntary associational relationship, there was no showing here that individuals within the named class see themselves as members of a group. Yet another failure, the Board said, was that she had not shown "women are expected by society to be abused, or that there are any adverse societal consequences to women or their husbands if the women are not abused." The Board then added, "[t]he factors we look to in this case, beyond *Acosta*'s immutableness [sic] test, are not prerequisites, and we do not rule out the use of additional considerations . . . But these factors are . . . appropriate . . . for consideration . . ."

The Board denied asylum on one other ground. Even if it were to characterize the described class as a social group, the Board concluded, there was no evidence that the applicant's husband would harm her *because of* her membership in that group.

Board member Guendelsberger, writing for the five dissenters, emphasized the soundness of the *Acosta* view, its strong reception in the U.S. courts of appeals and overseas, and its compatibility with fundamental norms of international human rights law. Following *Acosta*, the dissenters said, one could define all Guatemalan women as a social group. As for the majority's conclusion that in any event the applicant would not be persecuted because of her membership in the claimed social group, the dissenters pointed to several instances of specifically gender-related abuse. These included violent kicks to her genital area, repeated rapes, and attempts to abort her pregnancy by kicks to the stomach. Under those circumstances, it is not clear what the majority understood the statutory phrase "on account of" to mean. For a suggested causal approach, see the material on casebook pages 844-47.

At this writing, the decision in *R-A-* is still hot off the press. It is difficult to predict how wide its following will be. On the one hand, as you have seen in other parts of this course, United States reviewing courts often defer to the interpretations placed on statutes by the administrative agencies that implement them. On the other hand, while the application of the social group test to a set of facts requires judgment, the question of what basic test to adopt is one of pure law -- the type of question that courts seem more inclined to resolve independently. In addition, the *Acosta* test that the Board redefines has commanded a strong national and international following that courts might be reluctant to repudiate. Moreover, the Board itself was sharply divided; the final vote was 10-5. Finally, once the Board had applied the *Sanchez-Trujillo* test that bound it within the Ninth Circuit, it had done everything it needed to do. All that followed was dictum. In the light of all these factors, there seems little reason for courts to defer peremptorily to the Board majority.

Page 816, after item 7, add new item 8:

8. Pitcherskaia, the Russian lesbian described on page 815, has now overcome a major hurdle. The BIA had denied her claim on the basis that the Russian authorities did not seek to "harm" her; rather, they sought to "cure" her homosexuality through psychiatric means. The Ninth Circuit, holding that persecution does not require an intent to harm, reversed and remanded to the BIA for further consideration. *Pitcherskaia v. INS*, 118 F.3d 641 (9th Cir. 1997).

Page 817, footnote, before last sentence, insert the following:

Deborah E. Anker & Kimberly Dempsey, *Comparative Refugee Law: Gender Asylum*

Claims in Different Jurisdictions, 3 Bender's Immigration Bulletin 3 (Jan. 1, 1998); Joan Fitzpatrick, *The Gender Dimension of U.S. Immigration Policy*, 9 Yale J. L. & Feminism 23 (1997).

Page 827, item 5, 2nd paragraph, add at end:

In addition to the United States and Canada, Australia has issued Gender Guidelines. For a thoughtful comparison of the three sets of guidelines, see Audrey Macklin, *Cross-Border Shopping for Ideas: A Critical Review of United States, Canadian, and Australian Approaches to Gender-Related Asylum Claims*, 13 Georgetown Immigration L.J. 25 (1998).

Page 828, item 10, add at end:

Deborah Anker, Lauren Gilbert & Nancy Kelly, *Women Whose Governments are Unable or Unwilling to Provide Reasonable Protection from Domestic Violence May Qualify as Refugees under United States Asylum Law*, 11 Georgetown Immigration L.J. 709 (1997).

In a groundbreaking case, Immigration Judge John Gossart granted asylum to an Indian woman who had been beaten and threatened with death if she failed to pay her mother-in-law's continuing dowry demands. Judge Gossart found persecution on account of membership in a particular social group. He defined the group as follows:

> married Indian women currently past normal marriageable age in the State of Gujrat, who are required to live with their in-laws, that are unable or unwilling to acquiesce to multiple dowry demands of the husband's family, and are being beaten, dangerously abused and placed in trouble with the law as tactical blackmail, aimed at forcing the women's family to give in to the demands, and for which divorce is not an option, who are limited by their dialect and the need to be attached to a male (father, brother, uncle or husband) for protection to the region of where their family lives.

Matter of Patel, A74 974 011 at 10 (IJ Gossart, sitting at York, Pa., May 23, 1997).

The continuing viability of *Patel* is now in some doubt, however, as a result of the BIA's subsequent decision in *Matter of R-A-*, I.D. 3403 (BIA en banc, June 11, 1999). The latter case, discussed in detail in the Supplement passage adding item 11A on page 811, substantially constrains asylum claims based on spousal abuse. Do you think *Patel* survives *R-A-*?

Page 828, item 11, add at end:

See generally Deborah Anker, *Rape in the Community as a Basis for Asylum: The Treatment of Women Refugees' Claims to Protection in Canada and the United States*, 2 Bender's Immigration Bulletin 476 (June 15, 1997), 608 (Aug. 1, 1997) (2-part article).

Page 839, item 1, 2nd paragraph, add at end:

See Hope Lewis & Isabelle R. Gunning, *Cleaning Our Own House: "Exotic" and Familial Human Rights Violations*, 4 Buffalo Human Rights L. Rev. 123, 130-31 (1998) (describing the brutal conditions of Kasinga's detention).

Page 840, 1st paragraph, add at end:

Arthur C. Helton & Alison Nicoll, *Female Genital Mutilation as Ground for Asylum in the United States: The Recent Case of In re Fauziya Kasinga and Prospects for More Gender Sensitive Approaches*, 28 Colum. Human Rights L. Rev. 375 (1997) (applauding specific result in *Kasinga* but lamenting lack of guidance for future cases).

Page 864, 2nd paragraph, line 4:

Change "Court's" to "alien's."

Page 868, 2nd paragraph, add at end:

In *Matter of N-M-A-*, I.D. 3368 (BIA en banc, Oct. 21, 1998), however, a divided Board interpreted this requirement to mean only that the INS must prove that "the particular threat, which led to the past harm, no longer exists." *Id.* at 3. Thus, evidence that there is no threat from the applicant's "original persecutors" will rebut the presumption. *Id.*

Under proposed rules published by the Justice Department in June 1998, the issue raised in *N-M-A-* would become moot. Any evidence showing there is no reasonable possibility of persecution -- not necessarily evidence of changed country conditions -- would suffice to rebut the presumption. 63 Fed. Reg. 31945, 31949 (June 11, 1998), proposing to add 8 C.F.R. §§ 208.13(b)(1)(i)(A), 208.16(b)(1)(A).

Page 869, before last paragraph, add new paragraph:

The Justice Department has now issued proposed rules that would relax the constraints on discretion in cases of past persecution. Under the proposed rules, when there has been past persecution but no well-founded fear of future persecution, discretion may be favorably exercised as long as either (a) there are compelling reasons for the applicant's unwillingness to return or (b) there is a reasonable possibility of other serious harm (meaning harm other than persecution on one of the five statutory grounds). See 63 Fed. Reg. 31945, 31949 (June 11, 1998), proposing to add 8 C.F.R. § 208.13(b)(1)(iii).

Page 870, 1st paragraph, add at end:

On this issue, consider again the proposed Justice Department regulation described in the Supplement passage corresponding to casebook page 868, above.

Page 871, 1st paragraph, delete last sentence, and add new paragraph:

In the past several years, the Board seems increasingly inclined to allow immigration judges to deny asylum claims on grounds of lack of corraborating evidence, even as reviewing courts remind the Board of the obstacles faced by victims of persecution in procuring supporting documents. See, e.g, *Senathirajah v. INS*, 157 F.3d 210, 215-16 (3rd Cir. 1998). More generally, the Board has steadily increased its deference to adverse credibility determinations by immigration judges. For useful summaries and critiques of this trend, see Eleanor Acer & Beth Lyon, *And the Boat Is Still Rocking: Asylum Practice Update in the Midst of Shifting Regulations and Caselaw: Part Two*, March 1999 Immigration Briefings at 8; Harvey Kaplan & Maureen O'Sullivan, *The Role of the BIA in Reviewing Negative Credibility Findings: Circumventing the Well-Founded Fear Standard*, 75 Interpreter Releases 1181 (Aug. 31, 1998); Thomas K. Ragland, *Presumed Incredible: A View from the Dissent*, 75 Interpreter Releases 1541 (Nov. 9, 1998); Margaret Kuehne Taylor, *The Mogharrabi Rule in 1998: A Review of Recent BIA Asylum Decisions*, 75 Interpreter Releases 901 (July 6, 1998). Most of those decisions have prompted strong dissents, some suggesting that the Board's decisions on this subject have implicitly imported a legal presumption that an asylum claimant's testimony is fraudulent. See, e.g., *Matter of A-S-*, at 23 (Rosenberg, dissenting).

Page 875, item 1b, delete last sentence and substitute the following:

In *Matter of A-S-*, I.D. 3336 (BIA en banc, Feb. 19, 1998), the Board set out a 3-part test for assessing an immigration judge's adverse credibility determination when it is based on "discrepancies involving the heart of the applicant's claim." The decision will not be disturbed, the Board held, when

> (1) the discrepancies and omissions described by the Immigration Judge are actually present; (2) these discrepancies and omissions provide specific and cogent reasons to conclude that the respondent provided incredible testimony; and (3) the respondent has not provided a convincing explanation for the discrepancies and omissions.

Id. at 5. All three dissenters argued that that three-part test ignores the Board's responsibility to review de novo. See *id.* at 9 (Schmidt, Chairman, joined by Guendelsberger), 20-21 (Rosenberg).

With the advent of expedited removal, immigration judges now often have access to the handwritten notes of the interview conducted by the INS officer at the airport. In *Balasubramanrim v. INS*, 143 F.3d 157 (3rd Cir. 1998), the court held that the immigration judge had relied far too heavily on apparent disparities between the airport notes and the applicant's hearing testimony. The court recited countless deficiencies in the airport notes that made their content unreliable and reversed the BIA's affirmance of the immigration judge.

How should an immigration judge decide whether discrepancies -- either positive misstatements or omissions -- are significant enough to warrant adverse credibility determinations?

Page 877, 1st paragraph, line 5, at sentence break, add:

These reports are now on line, at http//www.state.gov/www/global/human_rights/hrp_reports_mainhp.html.

Page 882, 1st paragraph, last line, add a third provision to read:

INA § 208(b)(2)(B)(i).

Page 888, 1st paragraph, add at end:

For a criticism of automatic criminal bars, see U.S. Commission on Immigration Reform, U.S. Refugee Policy: Taking Leadership 33-34 (June 1997); Evangeline G. Abriel, *The Effect of Criminal Conduct upon Refugee and Asylum Status*, 3 Southwestern J. L. & Trade in the Americas 359, 369-71 (1996). Note, however, that for purposes of nonreturn, when a person has been convicted of an aggravated felony but not sentenced to five or more years of confinement, a finding of "particularly serious crime" is not automatic. In that situation, the seriousness of the crime is assessed with reference to the facts of the individual case. *Matter of L-S-*, I.D. 3386

(BIA, Apr. 16, 1999) (armed robbery of occupied home was "particularly serious"); *Matter of S-S-*, I.D. 3374 (BIA, Jan. 21, 1999) (importation of undocumented alien not "particularly serious").

Page 888, item 6, add 2nd paragraph:

The Supreme Court has now resolved this issue. In *INS v. Aguirre-Aguirre*, 119 S.Ct. 1439 (1999), the Court held that the BIA interpretation was entitled to deference, was "reasonable", and therefore would be upheld. *Id.* at 1445-46. The contrary position of the UNHCR handbook, the Court said, was "useful" but not "binding." *Id.* at 1446-47.

Page 897, last full paragraph, add at end:

Preliminary figures show approximately 55,000 applications filed with the INS in fiscal year 1998, and an end-of-year backlog of about 361,000. U.S. Committee for Refugees, Refugee Reports (Dec. 1998) at 5.

Page 914, 1st paragraph:

Note that the proposed regulations discussed in lines 3-9 are now final. See 8 C.F.R. § 208.4(a)(5) (1998).

Page 914, heading for subsection (2), delete the word "third."

Page 916, 1st paragraph, add at end:

Those talks have now officially terminated. See Press Release, Hon. Lucienne Robillard, Minister of Citizenship and Immigration [of Canada] (Feb. 5, 1998); 10 Int'l J. Ref. L. 256 (1998).

Page 916, last full paragraph, delete last sentence and corresponding citation, and substitute the following:

The Justice Department's regulations clarify that the person is then placed in regular removal proceedings for "full consideration of the asylum claim." 8 C.F.R. § 208.30(d).

Page 917, delete 1st full paragraph and substitute the following:

Some preliminary statistical data have now been compiled. In fiscal year 1997, when expedited removal began, about 79% of those who were given "credible fear" interviews were found to have demonstrated credible fear. In cases in which findings of no credible fear were reviewed by immigration judges, the affirmance rate was approximately 83%. See Charles Wheeler & Mary McClenehan, *C.L.I.N.I.C. Report # 5 on Credible Fear / Expedited Removal*, 3 Bender's Immigration Bulletin 411, 415 (May 1, 1998) [hereafter cited as CLINIC Report # 5]. Release on parole has been common for those people who succeed in demonstrating credible fear. A December 30, 1997 memo from the INS central office to the district directors provides that "parole is a viable option and should be considered for aliens who meet the credible fear standard, can establish identity and community ties, and are not subject to any possible bars to asylum involving violence or misconduct." *Id.* at 411-12. A 1998 General Accounting Office report gave the INS high marks for its implementation of expedited removal and recommended no changes. U.S. General Accounting Office, Illegal Aliens: Changes in the Process of Denying Aliens Entry into the United States, GAO/GGD-98-81 (Mar. 31, 1998).

Despite these positive signs, serious concerns remain. Some observers have noted major deficiencies in the GAO's methodology: The GAO failed to investigate several problem areas brought to its attention by others; it observed only 16 secondary inspections (the interviews at which INS inspectors at airports decide whether expedited removal applies and whether to refer the passengers for credible fear interviews); the GAO observed only 9 credible fear interviews and 5 immigration judge reviews; the GAO relied almost entirely on documents supplied by the INS itself; the GAO interviewed none of the individuals actually subjected to the expedited removal process; and the GAO made no attempt to discover the fates of those who had been returned to countries in which they had claimed to fear persecution. See Lawyer's Committee for Human Rights, Slamming "The Golden Door": A Year of Expedited Removal (1998); Karen Musalo, Deborah Anker & J. Edward Taylor, *The Expedited Removal Study: Report on the First Year of Implementation*, 75 Interpreter Releases 973 (July 17, 1998); CLINIC Report # 5, above.

CLINIC Report # 5 summarizes most of the problems that observers have identified in the expedited removal process. The outcomes of the expedited removal process vary a great deal from one district to another. In some districts, INS officials have made it highly difficult for the detainees to receive visits from family members or from attorneys. Interpreters are often incompetent. Interviews sometimes suffer from lack of privacy. *Id.* at 412-14. In addition, "[c]lients report being shackled to benches in airport holding rooms for up to 18 hours before being transferred to local jails or INS detention centers. During this time they are denied food and are separated from traveling companions or family members. As with all persons in secondary, they are denied the right to make a phone call." Wheeler & McClenahan, C.L.I.N.I.C.

Report # 4 on Credible Fear / Expedited Removal (Oct. 29, 1997). The INS has also been criticized for failing to notify passengers referred to secondary inspection that they have the right to apply for asylum. See Philip G. Schrag & Michele R. Pistone, *The New Asylum Rule: Not Yet a Model of Fair Procedure*, 11 Georgetown Immigration L.J. 267, 283-86 (1997).

Probably the most comprehensive ongoing study is a project co-directed by Professors Karen Musalo and Deborah Anker (see Musalo, Anker & Taylor, above). As of July 17, 1998, the project had gathered data on 280 individuals subjected to the expedited removal process. Its preliminary findings suggest significant *possible* discrimination on the basis of gender, English language proficiency, education levels, and nationality, as well as different outcomes at different ports of entry. *Id.* at 976-77. The researchers emphasize, however, that these patterns are highly preliminary. To investigate them further, they would need to observe actual secondary inspections. They report that the INS thus far has refused to permit them to observe and has withheld other needed information. *Id.* at 975.

As you have now seen, both the concept and the implementation of expedited removal have been highly controversial. The sources cited above have been highly critical. For other significant criticisms, see Anthony Lewis, *A Bad Time for Civil Liberties*, 5 Annual Survey Int'l & Comp. L. 1 (1999) (powerful attack, replete with concrete examples); Schrag & Pistone, item 1 above, at 1571-79 (criticizing expedited removal but offering positive implementation suggestions); U.S. Commission on Immigration Reform, U.S. Refugee Policy: Taking Leadership 30-31 (June 1997) (expedited removal should not apply to asylum claimants); *cf.* Maryellen Fullerton, *Restricting the Flow of Asylum-Seekers in Belgium, Denmark, the Federal Republic of Germany, and the Netherlands: New Challenges to the Geneva Convention Relating to the Status of Refugees and the European Convention on Human Rights*, 29 Va. J. Int'l L. 33 (1988). For other helpful commentary describing the workings of expedited removal, see Bo Cooper, *Procedures for Expedited Removal and Asylum Screening under the Illegal Immigration Reform and Immigrant Responsibility Act of 1996*, 29 Conn. L. Rev. 1501 (1997); Juan P. Osuna & Patricia Mariani, *Expedited Removal: Authorities, Implementation, and Ongoing Policy and Practice Issues*, Nov. 1997 Immigration Briefings.

Pages 917-18, delete subsection (4) and substitute the following:

4. Detention

Earlier you saw that certain aliens are detained while their admissibility or deportability is being decided. See casebook page 537 and the corresponding passages of this Supplement. Special considerations come into play, however, when the alien is an asylum applicant.

To deter people from filing asylum claims solely to prolong their stays in the United States, and also to assure the removal of those applicants whose claims are finally denied, Congress and the INS have increasingly resorted to detention pending final adjudication. There is no provision for detaining those who file affirmative applications, but those who apply for asylum in removal proceedings are subject to the same detention rules as any other aliens in those proceedings. Generally, they may be held without bond, released on bond, or paroled without bond. INA § 236(a).

The rules change, though, when asylum claims are filed by aliens subject to the expedited removal procedures discussed in the preceding subsection. If the asylum officer finds no credible fear of persecution, and the applicant requests that an immigration judge review that decision, then the applicant "shall be detained pending a final determination of credible fear of persecution and, if found not to have such a fear, until removed." INA § 235(b)(1)(B)(iii)(IV). The literal statutory language appears to contemplate detention even after an asylum officer finds a credible fear of persecution, INA § 235(b)(1)(B)(ii), but the INS practice has typically been to parole asylum claimants in that situation. See Charles Wheeler & Mary McClenahan, *C.L.I.N.I.C. Report # 5 on Credible Fear / Expedited Removal*, 3 Bender's Immigration Bulletin 411, 415 (May 1, 1998).

UNHCR has roundly condemned the detention of asylum seekers, absent exceptional circumstances found after individualized determinations. UNHCR Guidelines Relating to the Detention of Asylum-Seekers (Feb. 1999). The U.S. Commission on Immigration Reform takes the same position in cases in which credible fear has been found. U.S. Commission on Immigration Reform, U.S. Refugee Policy: Taking Leadership 32-33 (June 1997). The commentary has also been highly critical of recent INS detention policy for asylum claimants. In addition to the articles discussed in the Supplement passage corresponding to casebook page 537 above, see, e.g., Nicholas J. Rizza, *INS Detention: The Impact on Asylum Seekers*, 17 Refugee Rpts. No. 8, at 2 (Aug. 30, 1996) (describing the severe conditions). Others, while similarly deploring the conditions in which asylum claimants are confined, have additionally argued that detention tends to be ordered too often and for too long. See, e.g., Women's Commission for Refugee Women and Children, Liberty Denied: Women Seeking Asylum Imprisoned in the United States (April 1997); Women's Commission for Refugee Women and Children, An Uncertain Future, A Cruel Present: Women in INS Detention (1996), reviewed in 73 Interpreter Releases at 371 (Mar. 25, 1996). In *Kasinga*, I.D. 3278 at 9 n.1, the majority opinion criticized the INS decision to keep the applicant in detention as long as it did.

Pages 939-40, item 3:

(1) At the end of the 1st paragraph on page 939, add the following:

For the viewpoint of a U.S. Coast Guard captain, see Gary W. Palmer, *Guarding the Coast: Alien Migrant Interdiction Operations at Sea*, 29 Conn. L. Rev. 1565 (1997) (U.S. likely to keep searching for external refugee processing sites).

(2) In last paragraph of item 3, 4th-to-last line, before Costello citation, insert the following citation:

Irwin P. Stotzky, Silencing the Guns in Haiti (1997);

(3) After last paragraph of item 3, add new paragraph:

As discussed earlier (see Supplement passages corresponding to casebook pages 498 and 502), Congress in 1997 enacted NACARA, a broad statute designed to relieve &the immigration problems of designated Central Americans, Soviets, and Eastern Europeans -- but not Haitians. Believing Haitians to be equally deserving of special dispensation, President Clinton in January 1998 ordered temporary relief in the form of "deferred enforced departure" for Haitians who had been paroled, or had applied for asylum, before December 1, 1995. See 75 Interpreter Releases 2 (Jan. 5, 1998). As you have seen, Supplement passage corresponding to casebook page 502, Congress eventually passed legislation essentially codifying President Clinton's order. Haitian Refugee Immigration Fairness Act of 1998, Pub. L. 105-277, Div. A, § 101(h), Title IX, 112 Stat. 2681 (Nov. 2, 1998). Applications must be filed by April 1, 2000.

Page 940, after item 10, add new item 10A:

10A. Shortly after the Supreme Court decision in *Sale*, the Executive Committee of UNHCR issued a statement disagreeing with the decision, based on the language, structure, and purposes of the 1951 Convention. The position of UNHCR is that article 33 of the Convention applies on the High Seas. The statement chastised the Supreme Court:

> UNHCR considers the Court's decision a setback to modern international refugee law which has been developing for more than forty years, since the end of World War II. It renders the work of the Office of the High Commissioner in its global refugee protection role more difficult and sets a very unfortunate example.

UN High Commissioner for Refugees Responds to U.S. Supreme Court Decision in Sale v. Haitian Centers Council, 32 I.L.M. 1215 (1993); accord, Daniel J. Steinbock, *Interpreting the Refugee Definition*, 45 UCLA L. Rev. 733, 755-56 (1998).

Page 941, before the heading for section C, insert new section C, to read as follows:

C. CONVENTION AGAINST TORTURE

On December 10, 1984 the United Nations General Assembly adopted the Convention Against Torture and Other Cruel, Inhuman or Degrading Treatment or Punishment. U.N.G.A. Res. 39/46, 39 U.N. GAOR Supp. (No. 51) at 197, U.N. Doc. A/39/51 (1984), reproduced in 23 Int'l Legal Materials 1027 (1984), modifications in 24 Int'l Legal Materials 535 (1985) [hereafter cited as CAT]. The United States Senate ratified CAT in 1990, see 136 Cong. Rec. S17491-92 (Oct. 27, 1990), albeit with a long list of reservations, understandings, and declarations that are examined below. To date, American lawyers have made scant use of CAT, principally because until recently there was no legislation to implement it.

The landscape now seems certain to change, as a result of the implementing legislation finally enacted in October 1998. See Foreign Affairs Reform and Restructuring Act of 1998, Pub. L. 105-277, 112 Stat. 2681, Div. G, § 2242 (Oct. 21, 1998). From this point on, CAT claims are likely to be part of every refugee advocate's strategic arsenal. Some helpful commentary has already been published. See, e.g., Deborah Anker, Law of Asylum in the United States, chap. 7 (3d ed. 1999); Francisco Isgro, *Seeking Relief Under the Convention Against Torture*, 27 Migration World # 3 at 44 (1999); Kristen B. Rosati, *Article 3 of the United Nations Convention Against Torture: A Powerful Tool to Prevent Removal Just Became More Powerful*, 4 Bender's Immigration Bulletin 137 (Feb. 15, 1999).

CAT is the world's first multinational convention targeted specifically at the problem of torture and related cruelties. It requires the participating states to prevent torture within their own territories, to cooperate with other states by prosecuting or extraditing alleged perpetrators, and to do various things to protect actual or potential victims of torture. In addition CAT establishes a body called the "Committee against Torture," which has jurisdiction to investigate and adjudicate certain complaints of violations brought by individuals or states parties. As explained below, however, the Committee will play only a minor role in disputes that involve the United States.

Most relevant here is CAT article 3.1. It says: "No State Party shall expel, return (refouler) or extradite a person to another State where there are substantial grounds for believing that he would be in danger of being subjected to torture." Note the parallels to article 33 of the 1951 U.N. Refugee Convention.

Article 3.1 promises hope for some people who for various reasons are unable to procure asylum. Some are individuals who cannot satisfy the substantive criteria for asylum because the harm they fear is not persecution or because the persecution is not on account of any of the five protected grounds. Personal grudges, torture to extract information, and possibly certain gender-related cruelties are potential candidates. In other instances, CAT claims can possibly avoid some of the procedural obstacles associated with asylum. Conversely, as you will also see, there are situations in which an asylum claim will lie even though a CAT claim will not.

Because of various modifications introduced by the Senate during the ratification process, and because of some disputes concerning the precise effects of CAT, a brief detour on the law of treaties is necessary. Treaty law consists of both international law and municipal law. As for international law, the most important source is the Convention on the Law of Treaties, U.N. Doc. A/CONF.39/27 (1969), 1155 U.N.T.S. 336 (signed at Vienna, May 23, 1969), commonly called the Vienna Convention or sometimes the Treaty on Treaties. The United States is not a party to the Vienna Convention, but the State Department nonetheless treats it as "the authoritative guide to current treaty law and practice." See generally the clear description that appears in Mark W. Janis, An Introduction to International Law 15-39 (2d ed. 1993).

Treaties are negotiated in different ways, ranging from informal discussions among executive branch officials to formal conferences that often precede major multinational conventions. Some treaties, including both the 1951 U.N. Refugee Convention and CAT, were officially sponsored by the United Nations.

Importantly, the fact that a state has "signed" a treaty does not ordinarily make the treaty legally binding on that state. Signing typically indicates only that the text of the document is accurate. Janis, above, at 19. The treaty itself normally specifies what a state has to do to become a party; usually the state must communicate its ratification in a specified manner. In the case of CAT, a state becomes a party by depositing the instrument of ratification with the Secretary-General of the United Nations. CAT art. 25.2.

States also have their own constraints, imposed by municipal law. In the United States, the President presents a proposed treaty to the Senate, which may ratify it by a two-thirds vote. U.S. Const. art. II, § 2, cl. 2. Treaties that are ratified in this way become part of the "Law of the Land." U.S. Const. art. VI, cl. 2. But what effect do they have in a United States domestic court?

The answer is "it depends." Some treaties are merely contracts between states. The parties are expected to enact whatever legislation is necessary to keep their promises. In such cases a state's failure to keep its promises is a breach of contract, which the aggrieved state may pursue in the international arena. But there will be no remedy in a domestic court. Once the government passes the necessary legislation, a violation of that statute might well give rise to a legal cause of action in a domestic court, but such an action will be under the statute, not under the treaty. In contrast, in the United States and some other nations, domestic courts may directly enforce treaties that they interpret as "self-executing", i.e., not requiring domestic legislation. Whether a treaty is self-executing depends on the intent of the parties to the treaty. See Janis, above, at 85-86.

In the United States, a self-executing treaty commands the same authority as a statute. Courts will attempt to reconcile arguable conflicts between statutes and treaties, but if they cannot do so, the later in time normally prevails. *Id.* at 86-87.

Complications arise when the ratifying body -- in the United States, the Senate -- attaches conditions to ratification. These conditions take different forms. The most common condition is a "reservation"; the state purports to ratify the treaty but with modifications. Vienna Convention, art. 2(1)(d). This is permissible unless the treaty prohibits the reservation, or the treaty allows "only specified reservations, which do not include the reservation in question," or the reservation is "incompatible with the object and purpose of the treaty." Vienna Convention, art. 19. Depending on the treaty, a reservation might require affirmative acceptance by one or more of the other parties, or acceptance might be the default option. In any event, the reservation alters the obligations of the reserving state only as against those states that accept the reservation; furthermore, the alteration is reciprocal. See Janis, above, at 23.

When a state prefers not to make reciprocal modifications, it sometimes stops short of offering formal reservations and instead articulates its "understandings" or "declarations" of what particular provisions mean. Although it is the courts' job to interpret the law, they commonly defer to these pronouncements. See Barry E. Carter & Phillip R. Trimble, International Law 198 (2d ed. 1995).

With that background, it is now possible to describe the sequence of events that have made CAT a live option in the United States. As noted earlier, the U.N. General Assembly passed a resolution adopting the Convention in 1984. The United States signed it in 1988, the Senate ratified it (with reservations, understandings, and declarations that you will soon see) in 1990, and the President deposited the ratification instrument with the U.N. Secretary-General in 1994. See Rosati, above, at 184. Only at that point did the United States become a party. Implementing legislation was enacted in October 1998. Foreign Affairs Reform and Restructuring Act of 1998, Pub. L. 105-277, 112 Stat. 2681, Div. G, § 2242 (Oct. 21, 1998). In February 1999, the Justice Department issued interim regulations establishing the administrative machinery for the filing of CAT claims. 64 Fed. Reg. 8478 (Feb. 19, 1999).

The Senate declared that CAT is not self-executing, 136 Cong. Rec. S17492 (Oct. 27, 1990), Dec. # 1, and the BIA (before Congress passed implementing legislation) accepted the Senate's conclusion. See *Matter of H-M-V-*, I.D. 3365 (BIA, Aug. 25, 1998). At least one commentator vigorously disagrees. See Kristen B. Rosati, *The United Nations Convention Against Torture: A Self-Executing Treaty that Prevents the Removal of Persons Ineligible for Asylum and Withholding of Removal*, 26 Denver J. Int'l L. 533 (1998). Since Congress has passed implementing legislation anyway, you might be wondering, why does it matter whether CAT is self-executing? The answer is there are several respects in which the implementing statute, which reflects the Senate's reservations, understandings, and declarations, arguably falls short of meeting the United States obligations under CAT. If that turns out to be the case, nonrefoulement applicants will want to invoke the Convention directly; whether CAT is self-executing will thus become highly important.

CONVENTION AGAINST TORTURE AND OTHER CRUEL, INHUMAN OR DEGRADING TREATMENT OR PUNISHMENT

U.N. General Assembly Res. 39/46, 39 U.N. GAOR Supp. (No. 51) at 197, U.N. Doc. A/39/51 (adopted Dec. 10, 1984)

Part I

Article 1

1. For the purposes of this Convention, torture means any act by which severe pain or suffering, whether physical or mental, is intentionally inflicted on a person for such purposes as obtaining from him or a third person information or a confession, punishing him for an act he or a third person has committed or is suspected of having committed, or intimidating or coercing him or a third person, or for any reason based on discrimination of any kind, when such pain or suffering is inflicted by or at the instigation of or with the consent or acquiescence of a public official or other person acting in an official capacity. It does not include pain or suffering arising only from, inherent in or incidental to lawful sanctions.

2. This article is without prejudice to any international instrument or national legislation which does or may contain provisions of wider application.

Article 2

1. Each State Party shall take effective legislative, administrative, judicial or other measures to prevent acts of torture in any territory under its jurisdiction.

2. No exceptional circumstances whatsoever, whether a state of war or a threat of war, internal political instability or any other public emergency, may be invoked as a justification of torture.

3. An order from a superior officer or a public authority may not be invoked as a justification of torture.

Article 3

1. No State Party shall expel, return ("refouler") or extradite a person to

another State where there are substantial grounds for believing that he would be in danger of being subjected to torture.

2. For the purpose of determining whether there are such grounds, the competent authorities shall take into account all relevant considerations including, where applicable, the existence in the State concerned of a consistent pattern of gross, flagrant or mass violations of human rights.

* * *

Article 12

Each State Party shall ensure that its competent authorities proceed to a prompt and impartial investigation, wherever there is reasonable ground to believe that an act of torture has been committed in any territory under its jurisdiction.

Article 13

Each State Party shall ensure that any individual who alleges he has been subjected to torture in any territory under its jurisdiction has the right to complain to and to have his case promptly and impartially examined by its competent authorities. Steps shall be taken to insure that the complainant and witnesses are protected against all ill-treatment or intimidation as a consequence of his complaint or any evidence given.

* * *

Part II

Article 17

1. There shall be established a Committee against Torture (hereinafter referred to as the Committee) which shall carry out the functions hereinafter provided. The Committee shall consist of 10 experts of high moral standing and recognized competence in the field of human rights, who shall serve in their personal capacity. The experts shall be elected by the States Parties, consideration being given to equitable geographical distribution and to the usefulness of the participation of some persons having legal experience.

* * *

Article 20

1. If the Committee receives reliable information which appears to it to contain

well-founded indications that torture is being systematically practiced in the territory of a State Party, the Committee shall invite that State Party to co-operate in the examination of the information and to this end to submit observations with regard to the information concerned.

* * *

5. * * * [T]he Committee may, after consultations with the State Party concerned, decide to include a summary account of the results of the proceedings in its annual report * * * .

Article 21

1. A State Party to this Convention may at any time declare under this article that it recognizes the competence of the Committee to receive and consider communications to the effect that a State Party claims that another State Party is not fulfilling its obligations under this Convention. Such communications may be received and considered according to the procedures laid down in this article only if submitted by a State Party which has made a declaration recognizing in regard to itself the competence of the Committee. No communication shall be dealt with by the Committee under this article if it concerns a State Party which has not made such a declaration. * * *

* * *

(c) The Committee shall deal with a matter referred to it under this article only after it has ascertained that all domestic remedies have been invoked and exhausted in the matter, in conformity with the generally recognized principles of international law. This shall not be the rule where the application of the remedies is unreasonably prolonged or is unlikely to bring effective relief to the person who is the victim of the violation of this Convention.

* * *

Article 22

1. A State Party to this Convention may at any time declare under this article that it recognizes the competence of the Committee to receive and consider communications from or on behalf of individuals subject to its jurisdiction who claim to be victims of a violation by a State Party of the provisions of the Convention. No communication shall be received by the Committee if it concerns a State Party to the Convention which has not made such a declaration.

* * *

5. The Committee shall not consider any communications from an individual under this article unless it has ascertained that

(a) The same matter has not been, and is not being, examined under another procedure of international investigation or settlement;

(b) The individual has exhausted all available domestic remedies; this shall not be the rule where the application of the remedies is unreasonably prolonged or is unlikely to bring effective relief to the person who is the victim of the violation of this Convention.

* * *

Part III

Article 25

1. This Convention is open for signature by all States.

2. This Convention is subject to ratification. Instruments of ratification shall be deposited with the Secretary-General of the United Nations.

* * *

Article 28

1. Each State may, at the time of signature or ratification of this Convention or accession thereto, declare that it does not recognize the competence of the Committee provided for in article 20.

2. Any State Party having made a reservation in accordance with paragraph 1 of this article may, at any time, withdraw this reservation by notification to the Secretary-General of the United Nations.

* * *

* * *

RESOLUTION OF THE UNITED STATES SENATE RATIFYING CONVENTION AGAINST TORTURE

101st Cong. 2nd Sess.
136 Cong. Rec. S17491-92
October 27, 1990

RESOLVED (TWO-THIRDS OF THE SENATORS PRESENT CONCURRING THEREIN), That the Senate advise and consent to the ratification of the Convention Against Torture and Other Cruel, Inhuman or Degrading Treatment or Punishment, adopted by unanimous agreement of the United Nations General Assembly on December 10, 1984, and signed by the United States on April 18, 1988: PROVIDED, That:

I. The Senate's advice and consent is subject to the following reservations:

* * *

II. The Senate's advice and consent is subject to the following understandings, which shall apply to the obligations of the United States under this Convention:

(1)(a) That with reference to Article 1, the United States understands that, in order to constitute torture, an act must be specifically intended to inflict severe physical or mental pain or suffering and that mental pain or suffering refers to prolonged mental harm caused by or resulting from: (1) the intentional infliction or threatened infliction of severe physical pain or suffering; (2) the administration or application, or threatened administration or application, of mind altering substances or other procedures calculated to disrupt profoundly the senses or the personality; (3) the threat of imminent death; or (4) the threat that another person will imminently be subjected to death, severe physical pain or suffering, or the administration or application of mind altering substances or other procedures calculated to disrupt profoundly the senses or personality.

(b) That the United States understands that the definition of torture in Article 1 is intended to apply only to acts directed against persons in the offender's custody or physical control.

(c) That with reference to Article 1 of the Convention, the United States understands that "sanctions" includes judicially imposed sanctions and other enforcement actions authorized by United States law or by judicial interpretation of such law. Nonetheless, the United States understands that a State Party could not through its domestic sanctions defeat the object and purpose of the Convention to prohibit torture.

(d) That with reference to Article 1 of the Convention, the United States understands that the term "acquiescence" requires that the public official, prior to the activity constituting torture, have awareness of such activity and thereafter breach his legal responsibility to intervene to prevent such activity.

(e) That with reference to Article 1 of the Convention, the United States understands that noncompliance with applicable legal procedural standards does not per se constitute torture.

(2) That the United States understands the phrase, "where there are substantial grounds for believing that he would be in danger of being subjected to torture," as used in Article 3 of the Convention, to mean "if it is more likely than not that he would be tortured."

* * *

III. The Senate's advice and consent is subject to the following declarations:

(1) That the United States declares that the provisions of Articles 1 through 16 of the Convention are not self-executing.

(2) That the United States declares, pursuant to Article 21, paragraph 1, of the Convention, that it recognizes the competence of the Committee against Torture to receive and consider communications to the effect that a State Party claims that another State Party is not fulfilling its obligations under the Convention. It is the understanding of the United States that, pursuant to the above mentioned article, such communications shall be accepted and processed only if they come from a State Party which has made a similar declaration.

* * *

FOREIGN AFFAIRS REFORM AND RESTRUCTURING ACT OF 1998

Pub. L. 105-277, Div. G, 112 Stat. 2681
October 21, 1998

SECTION 2242. UNITED STATES POLICY WITH RESPECT TO THE INVOLUNTARY RETURN OF PERSONS IN DANGER OF SUBJECTION TO TORTURE.

(a) Policy.--It shall be the policy of the United States not to expel, extradite, or otherwise effect the involuntary return of any person to a country in which there are substantial grounds for believing the person would be in danger of being subjected to torture, regardless of whether the person is physically present in the United States.

(b) Regulations.--Not later than 120 days after the date of enactment of this Act, the heads of the appropriate agencies shall prescribe regulations to implement the obligations of the United States under Article 3 of the United Nations Convention Against Torture and Other Forms of Cruel, Inhuman or Degrading Treatment or Punishment, subject to any reservations, understandings, declarations, and provisos contained in the United States Senate resolution of ratification of the Convention.

(c) Exclusion of Certain Aliens.--To the maximum extent consistent with the obligations of the United States under the Convention, subject to any reservations, understandings, declarations, and provisos contained in the United States Senate resolution of ratification of the Convention, the regulations described in subsection (b) shall exclude from the protection of such regulations aliens described in [INA § 241(b)(3)(B)].

(d) Review and Construction.--Notwithstanding any other provision of law, and except as provided in the regulations described in subsection (b), no court shall have jurisdiction to review the regulations adopted to implement this section, and nothing in this section shall be construed as providing any court jurisdiction to consider or review claims raised under the Convention or this section, or any other determination made with respect to the application of the policy set forth in subsection (a), except as part of the review of a final order of removal pursuant to [INA § 242].

(e) Authority To Detain.--Nothing in this section shall be construed as limiting the authority of the Attorney General to detain any person under any provision of law, including, but not limited to, any provision of the Immigration and Nationality Act.

(f) Definitions.--

(1) Convention defined.--In this section, the term "Convention" means the United Nations Convention Against Torture and Other Forms of Cruel, Inhuman or Degrading Treatment or Punishment, done at New York on December 10, 1984.

(2) Same terms as in the convention.--Except as otherwise provided, the terms used in this section have the meanings given those terms in the Convention, subject to any reservations, understandings, declarations, and provisos contained in the United States Senate resolution of ratification of the Convention.

NOTES AND QUESTIONS

1. As the title of this Convention suggests, the drafters regard "torture" as a subset of "cruel, inhuman or degrading treatment or punishment." As the body of the Convention suggests, torture is seen as an especially virulent subset. The measures that CAT requires states to take with respect to torture are more stringent than those required with respect to "other cruel, inhuman or degrading treatment or punishment."

By way of example, states must take specific affirmative measures to prevent acts of torture within their respective territories, CAT art. 2.1, including criminalizing such acts, CAT art. 4. When torture is alleged, the state must either extradite or submit the case for prosecution. CAT art. 7. States must ensure procedures for torture victims to obtain compensation. CAT art. 14. Most important for present purposes, the nonrefoulement obligations imposed by article 3 apply only to torture.

The obligation to prevent and redress other cruel, inhuman or degrading treatment or punishment is narrower. CAT article 16.1 requires states to "undertake to prevent" such acts (by public officials) within their own territories, and it specifically makes articles 10-13 applicable to all cruel, inhuman or degrading treatment or punishment, not just torture. But those articles merely require states to include certain information in the education and training of law enforcement officials, investigate alleged misconduct, and provide a forum for complaints.

The phrase "cruel, inhuman or degrading treatment or punishment", or a very close variant, appears in other international human rights conventions as well. See, e.g, Universal Declaration of Human Rights, U.N.G.A. Res. 217A(III), U.N. Doc. A/810 at 71, art. 5 (1948); International Covenant on Civil and Political Rights, U.N.G.A. Res. 2200A(XXI), 21 U.N. GAOR Supp. (No. 16) at 52, U.N. Doc. A/6316, 999 U.N.T.S. 171, art. 7 (adopted Dec. 19, 1966); African [Banjul] Charter on Human and Peoples' Rights, OAU Doc. CAB/LEG/67/3 rev. 5, art. 5 (adopted June 27, 1981); American Convention on Human Rights, O.A.S. Treaty Series No. 36, at 1, OEA/Ser. L.V/II.23 doc. rev. 2, art. 5 (Nov. 22, 1969); [European] Convention for the Protection of Human Rights and Fundamental Freedoms, 213 U.N.T.S. 222, art. 3 (signed Nov. 4, 1950).

Our present concern is with the nonrefoulement prohibition of article 3. Since that article by its terms covers only "torture", the discussion from this point on will cover only torture, not "other cruel, inhuman or degrading treatment or punishment."

2. There are only two "reservations" to the Senate's ratification of CAT, and neither one is crucial to nonrefoulement. In contrast, Understandings 1(a),1(b),1(c),1(d), 1(e), and 2, as well as Declaration 1, are highly significant here.

In a moment you will have a chance to decide whether they are consistent with CAT. First, though, do you think it matters? Suppose the BIA, relying on one of the cited understandings and the declaration, denies a CAT claim. Assume the claim otherwise would have been granted. In a case that is properly brought, what should the court do (a) if the court finds that CAT is self-executing; and (b) if the court finds that it isn't? Before answering, consider not only CAT and the Senate ratification resolution, but also the subsequent implementing statute.

3. Read carefully the Senate's Understanding # 1(a), relating to mental suffering as a form of torture. Do you think this definition fulfills U.S. obligations under CAT? If initially it seems to fall short, does the second prong cure the defect? That prong covers "the administration or application, or threatened administration or application, of mind altering substances *or other procedures* calculated to disrupt profoundly the senses or the personality" [emphasis added].

4. The torture definition in CAT article 1.1 lists several purposes for which torture might be inflicted -- obtaining information or a confession, punishment, intimidation or coercion, and discrimination. Since the listed purposes are prefaced by the phrase "such purposes as," they seem merely illustrative, not exhaustive. The Senate committee that recommended ratification shares that view. See Comm. on Foreign Relations, United States Senate, Exec. Report 101-30, Convention Against Torture and Other Cruel, Inhuman or Degrading Treatment or Punishment at 14 (Aug. 30, 1990) [hereafter cited as Senate Foreign Relations Committee Report].

5. The torture that CAT article 1.1 recognizes must be "inflicted by or at the instigation of or with the consent or acquiescence of a public official or other person acting in an official capacity." What if a private individual or group inflicts torture and one or more government officials fail to intervene? Is this "acquiescence"? Senate Understanding 1(d) defines "acquiescence" to require "awareness" by the public official and a breach of "his legal responsibility."

The Senate Foreign Relations Committee Report, above at 9, says that the "awareness" requirement was added in order to clarify that even "wilful blindness" will suffice. (Does adding an "awareness" requirement really clarify that wilful blindness establishes such awareness?)

As for the "legal responsibility" requirement, at least one commentator argues, and the INS General Counsel's Office agrees, that "legal" includes international law and that the enforcement responsibilities created by CAT itself should therefore suffice. See Kristen Rosati, *Article 3 of the United Nations Convention Against Torture: A Powerful Tool to Prevent Removal Just Became More Powerful*, 4 Bender's Immigration Bulletin 137, 140-41 (Feb. 15, 1999).

A potentially more serious constraint is Understanding 1(b), which limits torture to "acts directed against persons in the offender's custody or physical control." In cases of government acquiescence in private acts, to which "offender" is the Senate referring? If it is the private actor, does the claim fail because he or she is not a public official? If it is the public official who offends by acquiescing, will Understanding 1(b) bar recovery, since the official does not have custody or control over the victim?

6. Note the second sentence of CAT article 1.1 (torture does not include suffering from "lawful sanctions"). The Senate Foreign Relations Committee Report, at 30, recommended the following Understanding:

> * * * [T]he United States understands that "sanctions" includes judicially imposed sanctions and other enforcement actions authorized by United States law or by judicial interpretations of such law provided that such sanctions or actions are not clearly prohibited under international law.

On the floor of the Senate, however, this recommended language was amended. The amended version eventually became Senate Understanding 1(c), which you should now review.

(a) Identify precisely how the recommended language differs from the language ultimately adopted.

(b) What practical significance do you think the amendment has?

(c) Do you see any circular logic problems in the 2nd sentence of Understanding 1(c) (the sentence that begins "Nonetheless")? Consider especially the qualifying phrase "to prohibit *torture*" [emphasis added].

7. Section B of this chapter dealt with asylum and nonrefoulement in the context of persecution. Recall that asylum under INA § 208 requires the person to meet the "refugee" definition of INA § 101(a)(42), under which either past persecution or a well-founded fear of future persecution will suffice. Under the analogous nonrefoulement provision for persecution, INA § 241(b)(3), and under article 33 of the 1951 U.N. Refugee Convention, only a future threat to one's life or freedom suffices; past persecution is not a basis for 241(b)(3) relief.

In this respect the nonrefoulement remedy established by CAT article 3 is analogous to nonrefoulement in the persecution context but not to asylum. CAT article 3 protects only against threats of future torture; past torture is not a basis for relief.

8. CAT article 3 prohibits refoulement "where there are substantial grounds for believing that he would be in danger of being subjected to torture." Senate Understanding # 2 interprets this language to mean that torture must be "more likely

than not." The stated explanation was that, as you might recall, the United States uses a "more likely than not" test for nonrefoulement in persecution cases. Senate Foreign Relations Committee Report, above at 10. Does Senate Understanding # 2 accurately interpret CAT article 3?

9. As you saw earlier, article 33.1 of the 1951 U.N. Refugee Convention prohibits refoulement in the persecution context, but article 33.2 expressly allows states to make exceptions on certain criminal and national security grounds. Exceptions along these lines (though arguably broader than what the 1951 Convention authorizes) also appear in the United States implementing legislation. INA § 241(b)(3)(B). These were discussed in section B.5 of chapter 9 of the casebook.

CAT article 3, in sharp contrast to article 33 of the 1951 U.N. Refugee Convention, makes the prohibition on refoulement absolute. It allows no exceptions. The BIA appears to share that view, see *Matter of H-M-V-*, I.D. 3365 at 3 (BIA, Aug. 25, 1998) (dictum), as does the INS. 64 Fed. Reg. 8478, 8481 (Feb. 19, 1999). International law, including decisions of the Committee Against Torture, take a similar view. See Rosati, above, at 143-44. Even the Senate ratification resolution, which weakens the Convention in so many ways that you have already seen, makes no attempt to engraft criminal or national security exceptions onto article 3.

The implementing statute, however, raises the issue. Section 2242(b) requires "the appropriate agencies" to issue regulations implementing U.S. obligations under CAT. Section 2242(c) then says:

> To the maximum extent consistent with the obligations of the United States under the Convention, * * * the regulations described in subsection (b) shall exclude from the protection of such regulations aliens described in [INA § 241(b)(3)(B)].

Since the Convention doesn't permit *any* exceptions to the bar on refoulement, the qualifying opening phrase would seem to render subsection 2242(c) a nullity. This provision thus posed a dilemma for the Justice Department. If its regulations truly excluded the 241(b)(3)(B) aliens from protection, the regulations would surely violate United States obligations under CAT. For the same reason they would exceed the authority conferred by section 2242(c) above, given the opening qualifier. But if the regulations made no special provision at all for the 241(b)(3)(B) aliens, the Department would risk the political ire of Congress.

The solution was to issue interim regulations that distinguish "withholding of removal" (the usual remedy) from "deferral of removal" (a more limited remedy for 241(b)(3)(B) aliens). Both remedies prohibit refoulement for as long as there are substantial grounds to believe the person is in danger of torture, but the latter makes it procedurally less cumbersome to refoule the person once the danger subsides. The procedures are discussed more fully in item 13 below.

If the interim regulations were to change, and the Justice Department were to begin returning 241(b)(3)(B) aliens in circumstances in which CAT prohibits refoulement, the regulations would be vulnerable to challenge under the opening phrase of section 2242(c). In such an event, some difficult issues of judicial power would arise. These are discussed in item 14 below.

10. In *Sale v. Haitian Centers Council*, reproduced and discussed on pages 922-38 above, the Supreme Court interpreted the nonrefoulement provisions of both the 1951 U.N. Refugee Convention and the United States statute [now INA § 241(b)(3)] as being inapplicable to aliens intercepted on the high seas. But compare the language of INA § 241(b)(3) with that of the CAT implementing statute, in particular section 2242(a). Is *Sale* applicable to CAT claims?

11. Based on what you have read so far, what do you see as the practical significance of CAT article 3 for aliens in the United States? Invent one or more hypotheticals in which an asylum claim might fail while a CAT claim based on the same facts might succeed.

12. Conversely, is it possible for a CAT claim to fail but for an asylum claim based on the same facts to succeed?

13. The procedures for filing and adjudicating CAT claims are laid out in the Justice Department's interim regulations. 64 Fed. Reg. 8478 (Mar. 23, 1999). They essentially incorporate the existing procedures for asylum claims. *Id.* at 8487, amending 8 C.F.R. § 208.1(a). Even the same application form -- the familiar I-589 -- is prescribed for CAT claims, so that asylum and CAT requests can be made and decided together. The asylum-related provisions of the expedited removal process, which were discussed on pages 916-17 of the casebook and in the corresponding passages of this Supplement, also apply equally to CAT claims, except that "credible fear of persecution" becomes "credible fear of torture." 64 Fed. Reg. at 8479. Note that nonrefoulement claims, unlike asylum claims, are not subject to a one-year (or any other) filing deadline.

The one major procedural difference between CAT claims and persecution-based claims stems from the statutory constraint discussed in item 9 above. The CAT implementing statute, in section 2242(c), commands the administration to deny protection to aliens described in INA § 241(b)(3)(B) (those who are ineligible for asylum because of crime, persecution, or national security concerns), "to the maximum extent consistent with the obligations of the United States under the Convention." Since the nonrefoulement obligations under CAT are not subject to any exceptions, the Justice Department recognized it could not deny all protection, even to 241(b)(3)(B) aliens. It therefore distinguished two protective remedies -- "withholding of removal" and a slightly less favorable remedy called "deferral of removal." The former is for aliens who satisfy all the requirements of CAT and do not fall within any of the 241(b)(3)(B) disqualifications. The latter is for those who meet the CAT requirements but fall within one of the 241(b)(3)(B) disqualifications. The application for withholding is deemed to include an alternative application for deferral; thus, the latter will automatically be granted if the 241(b)(3)(B) disqualifications are the only reason for denying withholding. 64 Fed. Reg. at 8481.

Both remedies bar the person's return to the country in which torture is feared but, like the persecution-related form of nonrefoulement that you studied earlier, neither remedy prevents the INS from returning the person to a safe third country. The asylum rules that govern detention and employment authorization while proceedings are pending apply here as well.

The main difference between withholding and deferral concerns the ease of termination. To terminate withholding of removal, the INS must move to reopen, produce new evidence that was previously unavailable, and sustain the burden of proving by a preponderance of the evidence that the alien will not be tortured. In contrast, to terminate deferral of removal, the INS need only move for a hearing and produce relevant evidence not previously considered. The immigration judge will then hold an expedited hearing at which the alien will have the burden of proof. An order terminating either withholding or deferral is appealable to the BIA. See 64 Fed. Reg. at 8481-82.

14. The implementing statute, in section 2242(d), addresses the subject of judicial review. Please review that paragraph carefully at this time. Dissected, the provision consists of a "notwithstanding" clause, then an "except" clause, then a clause that speaks to the reviewability of the regulations themselves, then a pair of clauses dealing with the reviewability of the denials of individual claims, and finally another "except" clause -- all in one breathtaking sentence. See some highly insightful parsing in Kristen Rosati's article, cited in item 5 above, at 145-46.

a. Is the INA § 242 petition for review procedure the only mechanism the courts may use to review denials of claims under the Convention or the implementing statute? In answering this question, consider both (i) the language that deals with review of "claims raised under the Convention" or the statute; and (ii) the "notwithstanding" clause at the beginning of the provision. As for the latter, is the "notwithstanding" clause absolute, or is habeas corpus available when no other form of review is?

b. Suppose the BIA denies a CAT claim on the basis of something contained in the regulations, and the applicant files a petition for review of the resulting removal order. Suppose further that the court believes that the regulations exceeded the authority conferred by the statute. May the court reverse the BIA decision on the ground that the regulations on which it was based were invalid? (Watch the statutory punctuation.)

c. The first "except" clause, near the beginning of the provision, purports to empower the Attorney General to decide, in the regulations, whether a court will have jurisdiction to review those regulations. The subsequent interim regulations say only that, pursuant to the statute, "there shall be no judicial appeal or review of any action, decision, or claim raised under the Convention or [section 2242(d], except as part of the review of a final order of removal [under INA § 242] . . ." 64 Fed. Reg. at 8492, adding 8 C.F.R. § 208.18(e). What do you think of the first "except" clause in section 2242(d)?

15. The procedures you have been considering are provided by United States municipal law. CAT also establishes some international remedies in torture cases, but as you will soon discover they will be of little use to CAT claimants in the United States, at least in the nonrefoulement context. To see why this is so, review CAT articles 20, 21, and 22 (which deal with three different powers of the Committee Against Torture), then CAT article 28, and then Declaration # 2 of the Senate ratification resolution. Exactly which competencies of the Committee Against Torture does the United States accept?

16. CAT Article 30.1 creates another international dispute resolution mechanism. If states parties disagree about the interpretation or application of CAT and cannot resolve the dispute through negotiation, any one of them may submit the case to arbitration. If after six months the parties cannot agree on the organization of the arbitration, then any of them may refer the case to the International Court of Justice (ICJ) in the Hague. Article 30.2, however, allows any State Party to opt out of article 30.1. In Reservation # 2 of the Senate ratification resolution, the United States did so. The Senate Foreign Relations Committee Report, at 28, explained that this decision was in keeping with the Reagan Administration's 1985 withdrawal from the compulsory jurisdiction of the ICJ (in the midst of Nicaragua's suit against the U.S.).

17. As is probably obvious from the long list of reservations, understandings, and declarations in the Senate ratification resolution, the final product reflected compromises among Senators with vastly different views about human rights, United States sovereignty, and the whole concept of an international legal order. Some Senators wanted CAT to have real teeth, even if that meant that the United States, like every other State Party, could be held accountable to an international body. Other Senators staunchly opposed ratification and as a fallback position sought to make CAT as ineffectual as possible. Contrast the following speeches on the Senate floor during the ratification debate:

Senator Nancy Kassabaum (R-Kansas):

Mr. President, I rise today to express my strong support for ratification of [CAT]. * * *

Last July, Amnesty International released its 1990 report documenting the incidence of torture of thousands of individuals in more than 100 countries. Though we do live with the reality of state-sanctioned torture in some countries, as well as its random occurrence, amnesty's statistics were nothing less than shocking.

Our ratification of the Convention Against Torture will, in itself, lead us closer to the goal it represents. The convention makes legitimate the right of nations to be concerned and to intercede regarding the behavior of another country toward its citizens. * * *

* * *

Critics of this convention also say it may give other countries opportunity to make charges against the United States. I do not agree with this because I believe we have nothing to fear about our compliance with the terms of this treaty. Torture is simply not accepted in this country, and never will be.

* * *

Mr. President, I would note that the United States is the only permanent member of the U.N. Security Council which has not ratified the convention. * * *

The Torture Convention * * * would send a powerful signal to torturers around the world that the United States will not tolerate its practice. As we near the end of the 20th century, let us take this step to help bring the world closer to ending practices which deny individuals basic human dignity.

136 Cong. Rec. at S17491 (Oct. 27, 1990).

Senator Jesse Helms (R-N.C.), Chairman, Senate Foreign Relations Committee:

* * * [Here Senator Helms is speaking in support of a contentious "sovereignty" reservation that would have made CAT subject to the U.S. Constitution insofar as it is enforced against the United States.] [O]ne only has to look at the current membership of the Committee on Torture, which includes a representative from the Soviet Union and a representative from Bulgaria.

The Soviet Union and Bulgaria have their own particular expertise in the matters of torture. This Convention's Committee on Torture is a farce, and it may be a dangerous farce. One could well say in this case that the lunatics are indeed running the asylum. I do not want those folks poking their noses into the operation of the U.S. legal system. They have plenty to do with the notorious injustice exemplified by the two countries I have just mentioned.

* * *

However, since this Convention is primarily symbolic, it is not necessary to engage in a superfluous debate. * * *

* * *

* * * [I]nternational law is a mere subordinate agent to the U.S. Constitution. * * * A treaty is a contract between two independent parties; but unlike domestic contracts which are subordinate to the U.S. Constitution and customary law, a treaty is without sanctions other than the good faith, prestige and power of the contracting parties.

* * * International law is merely a combination of codification and basic international customary practice leading to expectations of action by a nation state, but it can in no way be determinative of any such act.

* * *

The Torture Convention is by and large a rhetorical gesture, expressing the revulsion which every decent nation has against torture. * * *

But if the convention is meant in itself to be anything more than a rhetorical gesture, or to lay the basis to go beyond a rhetorical gesture, then it may present a clear and present danger to U.S. sovereignty and to the people of the United States. When even nations notorious in the annals of torture such as the Soviet Union and Bulgaria, piously sign such a treaty, it cheapens the consensus.

136 Cong. Rec. S17487-89 (Oct. 27, 1990).

18. The Torture Victims Relief Act of 1998, Pub. L. 105-320, 112 Stat. 3016 (Oct. 30, 1998), is also relevant here. Sections 4 and 5 of this statute award grants to overseas and United States treatment centers for torture victims. Section 7 requires the Secretary of State to provide special training for foreign service officers on the subject

of torture, including gender-specific training for dealing with victims of sexual violence.

PROBLEMS

1. Police detectives in a totalitarian country have taken A into custody. Although they have no evidence that he has committed any crime, they think he knows the whereabouts of a prominent criminal fugitive. A denies knowing anything about the fugitive, but his captors do not believe him. After several hours of fruitless interrogation, his captors tell him that if he doesn't cooperate they will confine him permanently, and then one night in the next year they will kill him in his sleep. "Try thinking about that for a while," they tell him. They also tell him (falsely) that they have already killed his family. It has now been eight months, and A is still in detention. Has he been tortured (a) according to CAT; and (b) according to the U.S. Senate?

2. The secret police of another totalitarian country, acting on the direct orders of the President, apprehend and arrest B, one of the leaders of a peaceful democratic resistance movement. They detain him in a 4' by 4' jail cell. Every night the guards awaken him two or three times, beat him, and administer excruciating electrical shocks. He is given only enough food and water to stay alive and is never allowed to leave his cell. They tell him this treatment will continue until he signs a statement publicly renouncing the resistance movement and discrediting the other leaders by accusing them of fabricated crimes. B refuses. After three years in detention under those conditions, the President instructs the police to release him if he agrees to leave the country.

Emaciated, dangerously weak, and psychologically defeated, B agrees. Upon his release he obtains funds from the resistance, makes his way to the United States, and enters surreptitiously with the help of a smuggler. One week later the INS apprehends B and initiates removal proceedings. B applies for asylum and for relief under CAT. While proceedings are pending, B, desperate for cash, commits an armed robbery of a gas station. He is convicted and sentenced to five years in prison. (Note his offense is an aggravated felony under INA § 101(a)(43)(F)). In the meantime, the democratic resistance movement that B helped to lead has toppled the totalitarian regime and now leads a democratic government. Nonetheless the haunting memories of his imprisonment and torture at the hands of the secret police are overwhelming, and B wishes never to return. B is still serving his criminal sentence and the removal hearing is about to begin. Is there any relief for which B is eligible? Before answering, review INA §§ 208(b)(2)(A,B) and 241(b)(3)(B).

3. C, who lives in a rural region of a third-world country, has been relentlessly abused by her husband for the duration of their two-year-old marriage. The abuse has included dangerous physical beatings and violent sexual assaults, occurring several

times per month. Her husband repeatedly threatens to make the assaults even more brutal if she ever tells anyone or tries to escape. In any event, he assures her, he knows enough people that he could easily hunt her down anywhere in the country. Her screams and her conspicuous bruises make her situation obvious to all observers, including the police, but spousal violence is commonplace in her village and is routinely overlooked.

C escapes to the United States and applies for asylum and relief under CAT. Will she succeed?

[END OF MATERIALS ON CONVENTION AGAINST TORTURE]

Page 941, heading for "Temporary Safe Haven", change from section C to section D.

Page 944, last full paragraph, at end of line 4, add:

For a good summary of the TPS criteria and procedures, see Linton Joaquin, Mark Silverman & Lisa Klapal, Temporary Protected Status (National Immigration Law Center, May 1999).

Pages 946-47, delete paragraph that spans pp. 946-47, and substitute the following:

As of this writing, attorneys general have designated 14 different countries (Bosnia-Herzegovina, Burundi, El Salvador, Guinea-Bissau, Honduras, Kuwait, Lebanon, Liberia, Montserrat, Nicaragua, Rwanda, Sierra Leone, Somalia, and Sudan) and one province (Kosovo). In many cases the grants were renewed. Relief has typically been limited to people who arrived in the United States before the designation date. See Joaquin, Silverman & Klapal, above, App. I-D-1.

Page 948, 1st paragraph, add at end:

See now the NACARA provisions that cover Salvadorans, discussed in the Supplement passages corresponding to casebook page 498.

Page 949, item 8, add at end:

Professor Fitzpatrick's concern proved prophetic. There is now a lively debate about whether refugee advocates should favor increased reliance on temporary refuge as a strategy for persuading the world's receiving states to welcome larger numbers of refugees. See the Supplement passages corresponding to casebook page 766, item 2.

Page 950, 1st paragraph:

(1) In line 3, after "European", add "and other".

(2) In line 9, before the Plender citation, insert:

James C. Hathaway, The Law of Refugee Status (1991).

CHAPTER 10

UNDOCUMENTED ALIENS

Page 953, last paragraph, line 8, insert after parenthetical:

See, e.g., Kevin R. Johnson, *"Aliens" and the U.S. Immigration Laws: The Social and Legal Construction of Nonpersons*, 28 Univ. Miami Inter-Amer. L. Rev. 263 (1996-97); Gerald L. Neuman, *Aliens as Outlaws: Government Services, Proposition 187, and the Structure of Equal Protection Doctrine*, 42 UCLA L. Rev. 1425, 1428 (1995); Victor C. Romero, *The Congruence Principle Applied: Rethinking Equal Protection Review of Federal Alienage Classifications after Adarand Constructors, Inc. v. Pena*, 76 Oreg. L. Rev. 425, 426 n.4 (1997).

Page 956, last full paragraph, line 2, insert at sentence break:

See generally Evangeline G. Abriel, *Ending the Welcome: Changes in the United States Treatment of Undocumented Aliens (1986 to 1996)*, 1 Rutgers Race & L. Rev. 41 (1998) (describing shifts in enforcement strategy).

Page 957, 1st full paragraph, add at end:

A new border initiative in Brownsville, Texas, called "Operation Rio Grande," is discussed in U.S. Comm. for Refugees, 19 Refugee Reports # 7 (July 1998). Consider also the new biometric technology that the INS has summoned in aid of border enforcement. See Daniel M. Kowalski, *The $99 Border Guard*, 4 Bender's Immigration Bulletin 579 (June 1, 1999).

Page 957, 2nd full paragraph, lines 7-11, delete the two sentences dealing with IIRAIRA § 110, and substitute the following:

IIRAIRA § 642 went further, prohibiting all federal, state, and local government agencies and officials from restricting governments' or officials' exchange of information with the INS concerning anyone's immigration or citizenship status. In *New York v. United States*, No. 97-6182 (2d Cir., May 27, 1999), the court upheld the constitutionality of the federal law, ruling it did not violate the Tenth Amendment or the clause that guarantees every state a republican form of government, U.S. Const. art. IV, § 4.

Page 957, before last paragraph, add new paragraph:

IIRAIRA § 110 required the INS to start comprehensively recording the departures of all aliens by September 30, 1998, so that the INS would have the capacity to match each person's authorized duration of stay with his or her actual departure date. In that way, Congress hoped, the INS would be better able to identify overstayers.

Major problems ensued. In the United States, a high proportion of the border crossings are unrecorded, especially for Canadian and Mexican nationals with border crossing cards and for returning residents. As many observers pointed out, even if the INS had the wherewithal to perform the mandated task, the necessary procedures would paralyze traffic, disrupt trade, and wreak general havoc in border areas. Two noted commentators describe the problems well. See Stanley Mailman & Stephen Yale-Loehr, *The Price of Tracking Overstays*, 3 Bender's Immigration Bulletin 179-82 (Mar. 1, 1998). Several bills either exempting certain border crossings or delaying section 110 were therefore introduced. Ultimately, Congress agreed to delay implementation until March 30, 2001 for land border ports of entry and for seaports (but not for airports). Omnibus Consolidated and Emergency Supplemental Appropriations Act, 1999, Pub. L. 105-277, 112 Stat. 2681, § 101(b), Title I, § 116 (Oct. 21, 1998).

Page 958, after 1st paragraph, add new paragraph:

In July 1997, the INS Border Patrol and the local police of Chandler, Arizona (a suburb of Tucson) combined efforts in a massive five-day community sweep. Some 430 residents, all Latino, were arrested and removed from the United States. The Attorney General of Arizona wrote a highly critical report of the tactics, which included arrests based on nothing more than "skin color or Mexican appearance or use of the Spanish language." See Nadine Wettstein, *The Chandler Raids: Wake-Up Call or Harbinger of Local Police Enforcement of the INA?*, 3 Bender's Immigration Bulletin 101 (Feb. 1, 1998). Recall also the discussion on vehicle stops based on racial appearance, in the Supplement passages corresponding to casebook page 595.

Page 958, after 2nd full paragraph, add new paragraph:

Some believe that the answer lies in restructuring. Many, for example, have suggested replacing the INS with two or more separate agencies, one of which would have only enforcement functions. See the proposals discussed in the Supplement passages corresponding to casebook page 2.

Page 962, last paragraph, add at end:

In *Noriega-Perez v. United States*, No. 96-70513 (9th Cir., June 9, 1999), a court approved the use of civil sanctions for document fraud. The alien had argued that separation of powers principles prohibit Congress from authorizing what is essentially criminal punishment and entrusting the trial to an executive branch tribunal rather than an article III court. The court held the sanction to be civil rather than criminal and approved the procedure.

Page 964, 1st full paragraph, line 4, 1st word:

Change "authorized" to "unauthorized."

Page 967, next-to-last paragraph, add at end:

Stephen H. Legomsky, *Employer Sanctions: Past and Future*, in Peter Duignan & Lewis H. Gann (eds.), The Debate in the United States over Immigration, chap. 6 (1998) (identifying benefits and costs of employer sanctions); M. Isabel Medina, *The Criminalization of Immigration Law: Employer Sanctions and Marriage Fraud*, 5 George Mason L. Rev. 669, 678-96 (1997).

Page 975, 1st paragraph, add at end:

In any event, at this writing employers have made very little use of the pilot verification system. 67 U.S.L.W. 2597 (Apr. 13, 1999).

The INS has not thrown in the towel, but it has shifted its enforcement priorities. It now plans to deemphasize employer worksite inspections and redouble its efforts to uncover smuggling rings and fraudulent identification documents. 67 U.S.L.W. at 2598 (Apr. 13, 1999); see U.S. General Accounting Office, Illegal Aliens: Significant Obstacles to Reducing Unauthorized Alien Employment Exist, GAO/GGD-99-33 (Apr. 2, 1999).

Page 975, 2d full paragraph, line 7, at sentence break, add:

M. Isabel Medina, *Employer Sanctions in the United States, Canada and Mexico: Exploring the Criminalization of Immigration Law*, 3 Southwestern J. L. & Trade in the Americas 333 (1996) (finding employer sanctions counterproductive).

Page 978, 1st paragraph, add at end:

The Second Circuit later held to the contrary, finding in section 1981 a cause of action for private alienage discrimination. *Anderson v. Conboy*, 156 F.3d 167 (2d Cir. 1998). For a good analysis, see Irene Scharf, *Commentary by Irene Scharf on Anderson v. Conboy*, 3 Bender's Immigration Bulletin 1102 (Nov. 1, 1998). The Supreme Court has now granted certiorari to decide this question. *United Brotherhood of Carpenters and Joiners of America v. Anderson*, 119 S.Ct. 1495 (1999).

Page 979, last full paragraph, add at end:

Note, however, that the EEOC and the OSC have now entered into a memorandum of understanding that makes each agency an agent of the other "for the sole purpose of allowing charging parties to file charges to satisfy the statutory time limits." The memorandum also permits the agencies to refer charges to each other when appropriate. 63 Fed. Reg. 5518, 5519 (Feb. 3, 1998).

Page 1005, after 2d full paragraph, add new paragraph:

In 1997 the district court entered a final judgment in *LULAC*. 997 F. Supp. 1244 (C.D. Cal. 1997). Before the 1995 decision, the State of California had requested a chance to draft regulations that would cure the defects in Proposition 187. The court, while skeptical that curative regulations could be drafted, granted the request. In the meantime, though, the Welfare Act passed. California then advised the court it would not attempt to draft curative regulations; Proposition 187 would rise or fall on its own merits. The court held that the Welfare Act reflects "the intention of Congress to occupy the field of regulation of government benefits to aliens." *Id.* at 1253. Accordingly, it entered a summary judgment invalidating almost all of Proposition 187. Only sections 2 and 3, which penalize specified forms of document fraud, and section 10, a "severability" clause that allows some sections to withstand the invalidation of others, survived.

The State of California appealed to the Ninth Circuit. While the appeal was pending, however, Governor Pete Wilson, one of the chief proponents of Proposition 187, completed his term of office. His successor, Gray Davis, was an opponent of Proposition 187. Everyone wondered: Would Governor Davis drop the appeal? To do so, he feared, would be a breach of his gubernatorial duty to uphold California law. To do otherwise, though, would jeopardize the education of hundreds of thousands of schoolchildren in ways that he (and the district court) believed were unconstitutional.

Governor Davis's solution was to request the court of appeals to invoke its special mediation procedure, in which the opposing parties attempt to negotiate a settlement. That request was controversial. Backers of Proposition 187 objected that the two "opposing" parties now in fact are of the same mind on Proposition 187 -- that it should be invalidated. They suggest that true negotiation will be impossible. Opponents of Proposition 187 were also taken aback. They would have preferred that Governor Davis simply drop the appeal. In April 1999, the court granted the Governor's request for mediation. See Bob Egelko, *Court to Mediate California Proposition*, Assoc. Press (April 26, 1999); see also Dave Lesher, Los Angeles Times, May 21, 1999) (Governor Davis announced he will not enforce Proposition's education provisions).

Page 1006, 2d full paragraph, line 5, insert at sentence break:

see also Peter J. Spiro, *Learning to Live with Immigration Federalism*, 29 Conn. L. Rev. 1627 (1997).

Page 1008, after item 11, add new item 12:

12. At present, for purposes of legislative apportionment, undocumented aliens are included in the United States Census count. See U.S. Const. art. I, § 2, cl. 3, as amended by Amend. XIV., § 2 (referring to number of "persons", unlike other constitutional provisions that refer to "citizens"); U.S. Bureau of the Census, *Enumeration and Residence Rules for the 1990 Census*, 1990 Decennial Census Policy Memorandum No. 12 (1987). The Counsel to the Senate immigration subcommittee has argued that this should not be the case. Charles Wood, *Losing Control of America's Future -- The Census, Birthright Citizenship, and Illegal Aliens*, 22 Harv. J. L. & Pub. Policy 465 (1999).

It is usually assumed, however, that undocumented aliens, being necessarily less visible, are systematically undercounted. The use of sampling techniques to supplement actual head counts, particularly for individuals who do not respond to initial surveys, would clearly enhance the accuracy of the count. But in a 5-4 decision that will have major implications for states with large undocumented alien populations, the Supreme Court has now construed the applicable statute as barring the use of even supplemental sampling for purposes of congressional apportionment. The Court's reading of the statute mooted the analogous constitutional question. *Department of Commerce v. United States House of Representatives*, 119 U.S. 765 (1999).

CHAPTER 11

CITIZENSHIP

Page 1011, 4th full paragraph, add at end:

Donald Galloway, *The Courts and Citizenship*, in Carnegie Endowment for International Peace, 2 Research Perspectives on Migration # 2 (forthcoming 1999) (citizenship-based restrictions in Canada); Kim Rubenstein, *Citizenship in Australia: Unscrambling Its Meaning*, 20 Melbourne L. Rev. 503 (1995).

Pages 1014-15, delete paragraph spanning those pages, and substitute the following:

The Commission on Immigration Reform opposed the exclusion of lawful permanent resident aliens from welfare benefits. United States Commission on Immigration Reform, Becoming an American: Immigration and Immigrant Policy 73-75 (Sept. 1997). The scholarly commentary has generally reached the same conclusion. See, e.g., the UCLA Law Review symposium issue on immigrants and public benefits, which contains articles by Professors Abriel, Boswell, Johnson, Legomsky, Neuman, and Reich. 42 UCLA L. Rev. # 6 (1995). (Citations to the individual articles appear on page 1008 above.) See also Nora V. Demleitner, *Power, Perceptions, and the Politics of Immigration and Welfare*, 14 Industrial Development & Social Fabric 9 (1998) (exploring link between immigrants' political power and their rights in welfare state); Berta Esperanza Hernandez-Truyol & Kimberly A. Johns, *Global Rights, Local Wrongs, and Legal Fixes: An International Human Rights Critique of Immigration and Welfare "Reform"*, 71 So. Cal. L. Rev. 547 (1998) (raising human rights objections to 1996 restrictions on public assistance for noncitizens). For a statement of the arguments for and against extending public assistance to immigrants, see Stephen H. Legomsky, *Immigration, Federalism, and the Welfare State*, 42 UCLA L. Rev. 1453, 1462-70 (1995).

Congress has now receded slightly from some of the 1996 welfare disqualifications for immigrants, mainly by restoring SSI and Food Stamps to certain immigrants who were already living in the United States on August 22, 1996 (the date the Welfare Act was enacted). See Balanced Budget Act of 1997, Pub. L. 105-33, 111 Stat. 251, §§ 5301-08 (Aug. 5, 1997); Agricultural Research Act of 1998, Pub. L. 105-185, 112 Stat. 523, §§ 503-10 (June 23, 1998). President Clinton has proposed going much further, repealing some of the restrictions for future permanent residents as well. See Esther Schrader, *GOP's Muted Response to Welfare Plan is a Telling Sign of the Times*, Los Angeles Times (Feb. 8, 1999).

Page 1015, 2nd full paragraph, after Bosniak citation, insert:

Victor C. Romero, *The Congruence Principle Applied: Rethinking Equal Protection Review of Federal Alienage Classifications after Adarand Constructors, Inc. v. Pena*, 76 Oreg. L. Rev. 425 (1997) (urging courts to apply to federal alien regulation the same strict scrutiny that analogous state regulation would receive).

Page 1016, 1st full paragraph, line 14, insert at sentence break:

Nora V. Demleitner, *The Fallacy of Social "Citizenship", or the Threat of Exclusion*, 12 Georgetown Immigration L.J. 35, 56-64 (1997) (advocating at least *local* voting rights for lawful permanent resident aliens).

Page 1016, 2nd full paragraph, add at end:

See generally Earl M. Maltz, *Citizenship and the Constitution: A History and Critique of the Supreme Court's Alienage Jurisprudence*, 28 Ariz. State L.J. 1135 (1996).

Allegations of illegal foreign contributions to President Clinton's 1996 presidential campaign have triggered attempts to ban all noncitizens -- including lawful permanent residents -- from contributing to federal election campaigns. One such bill, H.R. 34 (1998), passed the House of Representatives in 1998. See 144 Cong. Rec. H1764 (Mar. 30, 1998). The issue is still very much alive.

Page 1027, line 2, add at end of Schuck citation:

reproduced in 12 Georgetown Immigration L.J. 1 (1997).

Page 1029, item 9, add at end:

Arnold H. Leibowitz, A Time for Decision: Citizenship at the Millennium (Office of Refugee Resettlement, Nov. 1998) (citizenship rightly holds only modest place in U.S. history and culture).

Rogers Smith suggests that United States citizenship law has historically reflected exclusionary impulses. He believes these impulses have had both positive and negative effects, enhancing cohesion but running counter to the civic myths on which the nation was founded. Rogers M. Smith, Civic Ideals: Conflicting Visions of Citizenship in U.S. History (1997). Reviewing the Smith book, Peter Spiro calls this the "citizenship dilemma". Since return to the days of exclusion seems unacceptable, he argues, the nation-state seems destined to become a less important source of associative identity. Peter J. Spiro, *The Citizenship Dilemma*, 51 Stanford L. Rev. 597 (1999).

Page 1036, Problem 10, last 2 lines, delete the sentences that read "He is still alive. Like Mary, . . ." and substitute the following:

[Mary was born in Canada in 1953. In 1975, Mary's parents left Canada for the first time ever and moved permanently to the United States, where they continue to reside.]

Page 1036, heading, change to read:

JUS SANGUINIS AND THE CONSTITUTION.

Page 1039, after 1st paragraph, add new paragraph:

In *Miller v. Albright*, 523 U.S. 420 (1998), the Supreme Court had an opportunity to clarify the constitutional standards, but no majority rationale emerged. Under INA § 309(a)(4), a child born out of wedlock may not inherit citizenship from his or her father unless certain additional conditions are met (including legitimation, paternal acknowledgment, or judicial determination of paternity). In *Miller*, a child born out of wedlock to a U.S. citizen father overseas argued that section 309(a)(4) violates equal protection by discriminating on the basis of the gender of the parent. By a vote of 6-3, the Court denied the child's claim. Two Justices found a rational basis, rooted in the prevention of fraud, for the statutory distinction. Two others decided that the child lacked standing to assert that her father had been the object of gender discrimination. And the remaining two Justices denied the claim because the remedy would have been a grant of citizenship, which they believed the Court lacked the legal competence to confer. The three dissenters would have invalidated the statute on equal protection grounds. See Robert A. Mautino, *Commentary [on Miller v. Albright]*, 3 Bender's Immigration Bulletin 523 (May 15, 1998).

Page 1039, change footnote 4 to read:

Daniel Levy, U.S. Citizenship and Naturalization Handbook (1999 ed.).

Page 1044, after the long dash, add the following:

The INS, with quality assurance review by the EOIR, has since studied the granted cases in which criminal issues were present. The GAO then reviewed both studies and reported its (minor) recommendations. See U.S. General Accounting Office, Naturalized Aliens: Efforts to Determine If INS Improperly Naturalized Some Aliens, GAO/GGD-98-62 (March 1998).

Post-election surveys revealed an irony. Republicans were accusing Democrats of seeking to naturalize people liberally and speedily out of a belief that the naturalized voters were disproportionately likely to vote for President Clinton. Yet Republican Candidate Bob Dole ended up doing better among foreign-born voters (receiving 46%) than among native-born voters (receiving 42%). AILA, Immigration Policy Report No. 26 (1997) (citing CNN/Time exit poll). That result, of course, says nothing about how the candidates fared among *recently* naturalized voters.

Page 1054, 1st paragraph, line 7, replace Goldstein & Piazza citation with the following:

Eugene Goldstein & Victoria Piazza, *Naturalization, Dual Citizenship and Retention of Foreign Citizenship*, 75 Interpreter Releases 1613 and App. I at 1629-32 (Nov. 23, 1998).

Page 1054, 2nd paragraph, line 3, after word "See", insert:

Tomas Hammar, Democracy and the Nation State, chs. 5-7 (1990);

Page 1054, 2nd paragraph, 4th-to-last line, delete "Hammar, above, at 81-83. See also" and substitute the following:

Hammar, in Brubaker above, at 81; see also Jorge Vargas, *Dual Nationality for Mexicans*, 35 San Diego L. Rev. 823 (1998);

Page 1055, 1st full paragraph, line 8, delete "forthcoming 1997" and substitute the following:

46 Emory L.J. 1411 (1997). For another strong defense, see Peter H. Schuck, *Plural Citizenships*, in Peter H. Schuck, Citizens, Strangers, and In-Betweens: Essays on Immigration and Citizenship, ch. 10 (1998).

Page 1055, last paragraph in subsection 3, add at end:

See also Convention Relating to the Status of Stateless Persons (entered into force June 6, 1960) and Convention on the Reduction of Statelessness (in force Dec. 13, 1975), 17 Refugee Survey Q. 101, 103 (1998).

Page 1070, item 10, add at end:

Christopher L. Eisgruber, *Birthright Citizenship and the Constitution*, 72 NYU L. Rev. 54 (1997) (arguing government should be responsive to, and thus 14th Amendment citizenship clause should be construed to cover, all people over whom government exercises jurisdiction).

Page 1072, 4th full paragraph, add at end:

For a thoughtful discussion of the entire problem, see Daniel Levy, *Administrative Denaturalization: Practical Issues under New Standards*, 74 Interpreter Releases 1701 (Nov. 7, 1997).

In *Gorbach v. Reno*, No. 98-35723 (9th Cir., June 4, 1999), the court upheld administrative denaturalization, finding that the Attorney General's inherent power to reopen her own decisions did not violate the statutory scheme. In reaching that conclusion, however, the court noted that de novo judicial review remained available. The district court had found the issue close enough to warrant a preliminary injunction, which the court of appeals terminated. The court of appeals did not reach any constitutional issues, since none had been addressed by the district court.

Page 1107, item 10, add at end:

For a highly useful analysis, see David M. Hudson, *Tax Problems for Departing Aliens*, March 1997 Immigration Briefings.

Other sanctions for tax expatriates are also possible. The Internal Revenue Code now prescribes the posting of the names of citizenship renouncers in the Federal Register. 26 U.S.C. § 6039G(e). For a sample, see 64 Fed. Reg. 3339 (Jan. 21, 1999). Another approach is offered in Jeffrey M. Colon, *Changing U.S. Tax Jurisdiction: Expatriates, Immigrants, and the Need for a Coherent Tax Policy*, 34 San Diego L. Rev. 1 (1997) (advocating "mark-to-market" approach that would tax expatriates on accrued gains and losses).